UGLY DUCKLING PRESSE :: DOSSIER

Common Place
© 2015 Rob Halpern

Distributed to the trade by
SPD / Small Press Distribution
spdbooks.org

Ugly Duckling Presse
The Old American Can Factory
232 Third Street #E-303
Brooklyn, NY 11215
uglyducklingpresse.org

Design and composition by goodutopian
Typeset in Arno and Avenir
Printed and bound at McNaughton & Gunn

The images on the cover and on the title page are based on
"SPRINT" (2008) by Arnold Kemp, used courtesy of the artist.

ISBN 978-1-937027-38-4
First Edition, First Printing

Funded in part by a grant from
the National Endowment for the Arts

Rob Halpern **COMMON PLACE**

"common place," "that which we cannot not see," etc.

—George Oppen

CONTENTS

A Square, a Cell, a Sentence   11

Hoc Est Corpus   21

House-Scrub, or After Porn   35

Hocus-Pocus (1)   45

Hocus-Pocus (2)   63

Correspondences   99

Late Night Emissions   107

Abundance Washed   125

Nocturnal Residua   133

To Burn with Love   145

Postscript: Devotional Kink   155

Acknowledgments   164

COMMON PLACE

Rob Halpern

A SQUARE, A CELL, A SENTENCE

this blank resource whose waste excels, a darker place where bodies bend, ribs break in vaster banks, my blunting force, just say whose organ, say whose bone, drafting futures, time negated & not perceived as use, being raw, the stone, the teeth, what strange glamour, hangs like a sun, this deciduous mulch, his skin, the sky, the latch, the bone

in saying all this, let's say I've acquired a kind of money function, or what stands in for that, I —

•

being of sound no prophecy feels, what the mind stands in for, fallout from the coined relation, the working day as a unit of measure, a calculable truth in whose place stands my dutiful fuck, love's dirty interior, the fur-bound corn, my sickly seed —

this eternity of stars repeating, whatever you make me swallow I'll swallow, I say, hearing it again, imagining the stone, his eyes like summer signs, suns of nature mask the place of meanest meat, a blank concealed in every sentence

•

everything takes revenge on time, like debt, this surplus of dead, my living décor, I swear on his balls, my very own sucking stones, or coins, a hardening of war and sex, the work of human food, whatever skins intelligence, rude, like fate, such rueful afterglow of what demise, mourning the passing of system-wide reference, this allegory from which no soldier's cock can be redeemed, deluge in which we find & fade

— such blips, sublime oblivions lurk, my whole interior being one with their optics

•

my money scored to other scenes, this dreamy residue, an aura of strangeness clings to his limb, a thing no longer here, a plain where sheep-walks haunt my desire for landscape, drowning dreams of nature as if the problem were one of acreage, or ground rent, not being retinal, profit turns up in my stool

— inside this scene, pure property of the deceased, for want of luster, harvesting vacancies in which I'd have a share, if only he would kiss my mouth, plant his metal here

•

whose meat exposed for channel jamming, whatever it takes to conduct pure signal, the body clogging up no frame at all —

while hot lust fans, sheer weight the earth imagines, loins patch nerves the drill, these stones exchange for skin, the bone, the seed, the teeth, some pure emotion, like kerosene, or pomegranate, fiber of the stalk, the wreck, the phantom, I mean, my heart conceals an extremist core, being murderous, this puny mushroom, nothing refers anymore, all shares illiquid, no guarantee to resell

•

an exchange of coin, clean interior living, the fur, the wave, the wall behind which spread sublime fields, productive bodies get me hard inside the figures, yr deciduous mulch, meaning money, pure sound after periods of sonorous decay

all of them killed by abstractions nobody made —

inhabiting his thigh, singing it even, as if the destruction were too silent to know, wedded to limb turned to stump, this common place

•

a bone in my ass, where all future relation resides, if only I could feel the structure of marketable risk, or even its idea, the world entrenched inside his meat, worn lace, the latch

— to which I've attached my song, his fallen body, a ruse to cure the nation, an obstacle wedged deep in old utopian zinc, nothing empirical, the country wants to plug this dreamer's lewd cognition, a feel for fucking without touching anything at all

•

— along these interior roads, unmanned U.S. drones, my vast imagination, having led a mini-Tet offensive in the South, whose shabby portion gleams and sewage glows, our one true possibility, being false

beyond fascination, so excessively lit, as if there were light in desolate cells, vision, being a security measure, like common meat still longing for transport —

just say the word *usufruct* and levitate

•

his body, this omen to be waiting for, source of clarity, a figure traced in stars, the bone, the lace, the tooth, the sky, in whose shadow I go on believing in myself, succumbing to old means, conditions under which I've prepared these communications —

HOC EST CORPUS

[────────] a civilian detainee, was found unresponsive with a ligature around his neck in his cell at the Behavior Health Unit (BHU), Joint Task Force Guantanamo Bay, Cuba, at approximately 2200 hours on (b)(6) 2009. The ligature was cut and resuscitation efforts were started immediately in the cell and continued at the local medical treatment facility. All efforts failed to revive him. He was pronounced dead at 2259 hours. (b)(6) medical records reveal a long history of adjustment disorder, anti-social personality disorder and stressors of confinement. He had a history of suicide ideations and multiple failed suicide attempts. He was on hunger strike since January 2009 and enteraly fed. The case was under investigation by the Naval Criminal Investigative Service (NCIS). Authorization for Autopsy: Office of the Armed Forces Medical Examiner. IAW Title 10 US Code 1471. Identification: (b)(6) is identified by visual recognition and his detainee identification tags. Fingerprints are obtained by NCIS and a tissue sample is collected for DNA identification, if needed. Cause of Death: Asphyxia due to ligature strangulation. Manner of Death: Suicide. NCIS Preliminary Investigation: At approximately 2120 hours the decedent requested to speak to a nurse and asked for a sleeping aid. He was last known alive approximately 10-15 minutes later when he asked the guard to close his "bean hole cover," a sign that he was ready to go to sleep. He appeared, to the guards, in "good spirit" and did not appear upset. He was discovered unresponsive a few minutes later at approximately 2155 hours. According to preliminary NCIS investigation, while the shift guards were performing periodic checks on the detainees at the BHU, the decedent was viewed through the cell window and noted to not be breathing. He was seen on the floor of his cell, on his right side in the fetal position, and was reported to have been covered with a blanket with his hands and feet exposed. He was facing the right cell wall with head slightly tilted. The guards entered the cell and secured the decedent's hands and feet prior to placing him on his back. The guards noticed a ligature consisting of an elastic band tightly wrapped at least twice around the neck and twisted on the left side. The ligature was wrapped tightly and had to be cut (at the most twisted part) from the decedent's neck. It was removed in two pieces. No pulse or spontaneous breathing was noted. CPR was immediately started. Passive vomiting occurred during CPR. Medical Records Review: The available mental health records are screened by the prospector and the overseeing civilian medical examiner prior to the autopsy; see "Postmortem Examination". Screening of the mental health records reveals a psychiatric history of adjustment disorder, antisocial personality disorder and stressors of confinement. The decedent had a history of suicide ideations, suicide gestures and multiple suicide attempts by hanging, neck ligature, self inflicted sharp force injuries and frequent blunt force trauma to the head. On January 2009 he started a hunger strike and had been fed enteraly. He has been on a suicide watch at the BHU, where he is seen daily by the medical staff. He had five suicide attempts in May 2009. Ligature: The ligature is collected as evidence by the NCIS at the scene and examined by the prospector and the observing civilian medical examiner prior to autopsy. The ligature is almost identical to the elastic band of a white brief, medium size 34-36, issued to the detainees at the detention facility. The ligature consists of two segments, with a combined aggregate length of approximately 23 ½" and width of approximately 1". The smaller of the two segment measures 6 ½" in length. The ligature fibers are elongated and distorted at the junction of the two cut edges c/w the history of cutting the ligature at the twisted part. There are no bloodstains on the ligature. Boredom distracts and numbness disorients, but arriving at that period I become acutely aware of my body as I write. The word "ligature" excites me and my left hand begins caressing my thigh. Postmortem examination: The postmortem examination (b)(6) of (b)(6) is performed at the US Naval Hospital (USNH), Guantanamo Bay, Cuba or (b)(6) 2009, starting at approximately 1300 hours. Full body radiological studies are obtained at the USNH. Photographs are obtained by (b)(6) OAFME Photographer. Attending the autopsy as medico-legal observers are (b)(6), Medical Examiner (b)(6) and Special Agents (b)(6) from the NCIS. External Examination: The body is that of a well-developed, well-nourished male clad in khaki shirt and pants without undergarments; see "Clothing and Personal Effects". Fondling myself as I transcribe this report feels inappropriate, a move I ought to arrest. The feet are held together with white plastic flexi-cuffs and the hands are held together with black plastic flexi-cuffs. The flexi-cuffs are cut open to facilitate the completion of the radiological studies. The hands are covered in brown paper bags, secured by adhesive tape; see "Evidence". A blue colored plastic identification band encircles the right wrist. The height and weight noted on the identification wristband are 68" and about 120lb. respectively. I'd much rather be reading *707 Scott Street* by John Wieners, which is sitting here beside the report I'm otherwise mechanically transcribing. *What can I write about / to set my heart on fire?* That's Wieners. The body appears consistent with the reported height and weight. Rigor is present to an equal degree in all extremities. Lividity is present on the posterior surface of the body, except in areas exposed to pressure. Body temperature is cold due to refrigeration. The scalp hair is black, long, covers the back of the neck and is matted. I feel pressure on my bladder and my face feels hot. If I hold that phrase "hair is black and long, covers the back of neck" in focus long enough, the image of his body begins to cohere around it, an image in total isolation from its textual support. Vomit is noted on the top and back of the head. The facial hair consists of black mustache and beard. The forehead reveals dark small raised lesions; see "Evidence of Injuries." The eyes are unremarkable. The irides are brown. The cornea are slightly cloudy. The conjunctivae appear injected with no significant petechia. This is the first word I need to look up, but I don't have a medical dictionary at hand, only one for Latin, and no internet access here at home, no smart phone. The sclerae are white with no petechia. The external auditory canals, external nares and oral cavity are free of foreign material and abnormal secretions. The nasal skeleton is palpably intact. The tongue is unremarkable. The lips are without evidence of injury. What would it be like to kiss them? Transcription of the autopsy report gives way to these fantasies of contact. Every sentence arrives at its denotative limit in a body dead on a gurney, which having been withdrawn, carries with it the threads that connect it to a world, as if my own sentences possessed some restorative force to bring the body back. Is this the opposite of Bartleby's refusal to copy? As if, in writing, "The teeth are natural and unremarkable," the teeth would in fact be natural and unremarkable. Mention of his unbruised organs yields this rush to my adrenal gland. His matted hair *so limp with curl* my specimen on the table. To be penetrated is to abdicate every pretense of power. His death can't be verified except by a report that falsifies the flesh, only thereby making it true. Examination of the neck reveals a broad patterned impression on the anterior and dark colored impression on the posterior. The chest is unremarkable. But how can the chest be unremarkable? His chest can only be remarkable, inconceivable referent to which my love fails to cling. There's that default move of hand to cock again, an incorrigible tic. No injury of the ribs or sternum is evident externally. The abdomen is unremarkable. Each sentence remains wired to real force as the report resembles architecture, my distraction, this absent-minded orientation. No evidence of major surgical scars. The posterior torso is unremarkable with no evidence of trauma. A healing ¾ x ½" ulcer of unknown etiology is noted on the right lower back, immediately below the waist. I'm struck by the word "healing," the tense, indeed the word itself, conspicuous misnomer, as I imagine the origin of this scar, the mouth of a lover, a bit of metal, some kind of punch or jab. The external genitalia are those of a normal adult circumcised male, and unremarkable. I just lost my place in the document. I don't want to continue doing this tonight, but I'll keep it up, as if under duress, hah, a duration constraint. The extremities are unremarkable with no evidence of recent trauma. Linear broad impressions are noted on the right wrist and ankles, consistent with the history of use of the flexi-cuff ties. Multiple well-healed scars are noted on the right anterior neck, scalp, right arm, right shoulder, left anticubital fossa, left thumb, both knees, left shin and the dorsal surface of the left foot, photographed for documentation. Each of these deserves elaboration, fiction, love. No tattoos or other major surgical scars or identifying marks are noted. I think it's significant that I'm transcribing this sentence while listening to one of Andrew Hill's last big band recordings, *A Beautiful Day*, a disc I found at Community Thrift on Valencia and 17th in San Francisco several years ago at a moment when I couldn't get enough of Hill's compositions. My audition alters my mood, affects my concentration, and has me thinking of things only scantly related to the report I suppose I should abandon now. Evidence of Injury: Neck trauma. External examination of the neck reveals a ligature impression. A broad reddish discoloration is noted on the skin of the anterior neck, overlying the thyroid cartilage measuring 1 ½" at the maximum width on the midline. The ligature mark has a maximum width of 1 ½" at the anterior midline, and is slightly upwardly angled toward the posterior neck. The ligature impression is incomplete and fades and disappears below the ears. How to complete this impression? It's like as soon as the body comes into focus, it disappears, or proves never to have been there to begin with. Maybe this is the coroner's equivalent of the soldier's responsibility "to tag documents and other personal property taken so you know which prisoner had them," a line I am copying now from *The Soldier's BCT Handbook* (Department of the Army, May 1969) issued at the height of the Vietnam War, something I bought for 75 cents at the reuse store in Ann Arbor shortly after arriving in Michigan suspecting that it would come in handy, and I impulsively reach for it as if seeking the association. A small superficial abrasion is noted below the right ear (see "Opinion"). A thick dark linear discoloration is noted on the posterior neck (see "Opinion"). Dissection and examination of the strap muscles of the neck reveals localized hemorrhage on the right side of the sterno-hyoid muscle, underlying the above noted ligature impression and contusion on the right side of the neck. No other trauma is noted. Disavowal of what can't be noted. And so I, too, turn away from the signs that inscribe this body's truth, which doesn't exist anterior to the report that documents it. I can't help but wonder were I transcribing *The Phenomenology of Spirit*, would I still be moved by these impulses to touch myself? I mean, is the inclination to masturbate an effect of generic boredom or particular content? The hyoid bone and thyroid cartilage are still intact. Examination of the forehead reveals a small cluster of dark raised lesions, on the midline, in an area measuring ¾ x ½" with underlying mild subcutaneous hemorrhage and no underlying skull fractures (see "Opinion"). A fracture of the anterior right 5th rib is noted with minimal surrounding hemorrhage (see "Opinion"). A well-healed scar overlies a malunion fracture of the right humerus is noted [*sic*], consistent with remote unrelated trauma (firearm injury in 2002 per medical records). The incisions are photographed for documentation. I'm struck by all these passive constructions. Total refusal of agency, as if patiency were the environmental mood, a grammatical ambient effect. This is where the difference between a solider and a detainee breaks down, leaving me harnessed to liquefied features and redacted names, none of which can support my sentence. There is a superficial healing abrasion on the left shin. No other significant injuries are noted. Serial incisions on the back and upper and lower extremities reveal no evidence of trauma. As my hand reaches beneath the ligature that secures his Army-issued linen pants, I can feel the thick nest of hair as my fingers touch the head of his cock, which stiffens with the touch. But none of this is true, it's my own prick getting hard as this exercise in auto-affection turns blind figures to waste. Unlike my soldier, the detainee repulses eros, failing to sustain the referential illusion. Who needs virility enhancements when you can write sentences like these to overcome the intransitivity of certain verbs, the negation of relation itself. That's when his organs emit a ball of fire whose light is diminished by the nimbus round his floating corpse. His body, being the thing that holds us all together, must be the truth of the transcendental subject upon which every notion of justice rests. "A sign's incarnation in the body," reads a note I left for myself, and I wonder what I mean by this. The ligature must be the singular point, like the hook on which each universal hangs, the common place of my report, the particular that proves the whole false. This makes it difficult to endure my own procedure *hard to keep it up* the task I've set myself. After a few sentences, for example, each of which promises the security of stable reference whose phantom drapes itself in coy mystique, the naïvité of the autopsy's realism opens on a little cul-de-sac where my appendix dangles in somatic void, a common grave where proper names dissolve, the body itself redacted, wasted and withdrawn to a lockdown site I've stored inside my special cavity, beside the puny mushroom or heart. Taken literally, his body is unthinkable, a mineral fact suspended outside the only language wherein we might encounter it. Swarming in the language of report, his organs inseminate my sentence, make it sentient. How to feel the thing hovering just beyond effigy without falling to temptation, an opening to my mystified other. It's really Flaubert's Julian I want to be, the way he lies full length atop the leper, mouth to mouth, chest to chest, compassion being an act of the whole body. Every time I arrive at the end of that story, my eyes well up, so it's strange I'm not crying now as I cling to his figure as though it were my inner life. But I won't learn to mourn by covering my naked self with shit while reciting my poems for you. In order to arrive at love, I need to run straight thru disgust without stopping at abjection. I want to keep myself hard while doing this so that every line bears some direct relation to arousal. I remember

Delany writing something like this about *Hogg*, though it's not like that at all, as if transcription could animate the dead. Can I even call it pleasure when every phrase dissociates flesh and world, and sensation hangs on its total separation from the thing arousing this image of it? It's like the space between my body and his were equal to the space between me and myself. In other words, the outcome I'm intuiting is incompatible with my own preservation. Jerking off to the document may be the closest I'll come, from the comfort of my bedroom to the limit of what's speakable, whose unit of measure is one with the clinician's sentence. "The upper airway is clear of debris and foreign material." "The urinary bladder is unremarkable and contains clear yellow urine." "The esophagus is lined by gray-white smooth mucosa." It makes no sense for my hard-on to shame me, opposing the stiffness of his body. So at the limit of my fantasy, I use that velvety mucosa and falsely measured fat like a lubricant as every word makes me sing for the world we've failed to make, and I sing like a lark to the sun.

Armed Forces Institute of Pathology Office of the Armed Forces Medical Examiner 1413 Research Blvd. Bldg 102. Rockville MD 20850 1-301-319-0000 (FAX 1-301-319-0635) Final Autopsy Report. Name: Al Hanashi Muhammad Ahmad A.S. Autopsy No (b) (6). ID No. (b) (6). AFIP No. (b)(6) Date of Birth: Unknown Rank: Civilian Date of Autopsy: 03 JUN 2009 1300 hours Place of Death: Guantanamo Bay Date of Report 23 JUN 2009. Place of Autopsy: US Naval Hospital. Guantanamo Bay Cuba.

HOUSE-SCRUB
OR, AFTER PORN

THERE ARE SO many things I want to tell you, things that embarrass me most, though it's hard to voice any one of them, even for you whom I've come to trust. So far, all my writing amounts to these strategies of evasion. That's what I was telling Dana & Lee, sitting outside in the late August heat as we tried to grasp where it all might be going. Casting idols on my brain, the sun produces these false appearances, the dahlias burning under gunmetal skies, so I've yet to discover what real life feels like. At least that's what I tell them. But what I want to tell you is, well, take my body, for example, a place where incommensurables collide *rhetoric & blood, price & value, datum & event* the bad equivalent of a hole in a soldier's bladder before he's given the form to join the donor's club. The dialectic, having come to such dumb arrest, yields this taxonomy of wounds pasted to a straw man I'll never fuck, a cheap shot at militarization, its so-called human face. What figure do combatants cut against a company that earns the bulk of its twelve billion in annual revenue from army contracts, and whose product tracks my car as it moves thru any one of eight hundred Oakland intersections. This is why my book amounts to a simple X without the algebra to resolve its value in a world where the word "decorative" modifies unintelligible things, thereby assisting sales. As in every cash-starved city, the promise of federal dollars makes military surveillance an easy cow. See what I mean, in the absence of incident, structure eludes, the poem being but the gesture of a body groping its own withdrawn architecture. Whether bound or bundled, all my usable parts compress to the volume of a prosthetic device shoved inside a foreign orifice. This is how capital explodes in song, usurping the air you might be privately singing, the way the very idea of the flood dries up after the deluge. That's so dutifully Rimbaud, but what would the equivalent be? After the idea of collapse recedes, my use of disjunction will bear no relation to a break in the chain of title, a detainee's autopsy report, or any old forensic audit robo-signed & withdrawn in hazy spells of law. But nothing appears to accumulate inside the hole my organ makes when, mortally wounded in a grenade attack, his blown genitals get contracted to a public utility, a city square or park, this being but an asset to securitize, a convention by whose rhyme scheme "scars" and "cars" seem to be of common scale, a sound to sing no polis. Who can accommodate such rules when the totality penetrates yr colon, absorbs yr shit, the very thing that arouses my pleasure and can't be absorbed by narration, soothed by his big dead muscle. With the help of newly calibrated nite-vision goggles, we'll eventually retrieve what bodies will have been interred from yet another abandoned future [——] here among the low-slung concrete municipal buildings, location of my operative and verse. If the incompletion theorem is correct and any account of a logically coherent system must contain at least one radical instance that can't be contained by that account, then my soldier's wound must be just such an instance, a hole in sense, our common place, nonsite of suffering under current conditions, negative imprint of all my social relations, resistant to story though submissive to an allegory turned against the conceptual purity of its own redemptive function, bearing no resemblance to my form. Having mistaken securitization for security, whatever it is my body craves has already been sold as the normal way of belonging to the things that own me. With the sap that keeps me in bed with my financialized double, I adhere to the aggregate of productive labor hours necessary to repay what I owe, which daily exceeds my waking life. Ever since my last anonymous fuck, I've been feeling totally adrift in dark liquidity pools, thinking about Greece and Portugal, or my dad's diminishing bank account, though I can barely keep all this in my head, currency flux being the means to ensure my hope in retirement, the hedge around my bed being taller than I can scale, so many new instruments & futures, asset values expanding at 3% per annum as all my so-called friendships become sites of monetary extraction. With the outsourcing of such suffering, the meaning of my rhyme depreciates to the size of a soldier's impotent nut, upon which I've fallen in hard times. I mean, when it's the leg that gets enjambed by precision rather than a line of verse, these are the extremes to which one's gotta go to overcome the mind/body split, the truth of abjection being an effect of objective falsehood. So my poems patrol the perimeter of popular speech, the bodies I sing of, being militarized form, each sentence an enclosure, like the globe itself, this emblem of sovereignty, where our relations exist inside systems of yield and harvest, as organ and seed enhance the dearness of my product. Dying from this illusion of scarcity, each abstract universal fails the concrete assertion of material life, or remains excluded from it like his "esophagus lined by gray-white mucous." Who can out-perform the rules when the financial unconscious becomes a poltergeist, my house organizing appetite and shit in equal measure with my poem. Dead music on the floor, the time of life being anti-matter, a body pocked w/ decimals, distilled in a column of digits gracing page D6 where I've found love in bio-ruin while my body burns in each commutable decision to buy or sell. And as if to pass the time, or trick the labor that makes time real, I've taken to transcribing autopsy reports by hand, as if a conceptual procedure *any act of writing* could bring the bodies closer, or at least denote the wounds. This is how my soldier becomes a Gitmo detainee. I was cruising for army guys, but each visible scar is a portal to the same invisible disease, interminable detention and enteral feeding. I mean, how long can a body go on testing the load bearing capacity of militarized social networks wherein what needs to be negated are the conditions that enable anyone to declare "the subject is dead" by which I mean the Yemeni man whose name's been redacted [(b)(6)] at the top of this report, a civilian non-combatant found unresponsive with a ligature around his neck in a cell at the Behavior

Health Unit, Joint Task Force Guantanamo Bay, Cuba, at approximately 2200 hours on an elided date in 2009. But the so-called "subject" might just as easily point to a place in my poem, a form the body assumes in language though in excess of any grammatical position, like the one that binds my double to the private who'd replace him. Falling prey to nonsense, my writing denotes nothing but the apparatus that makes the corpus mean, a common grave, a ditch or sink, where ID fails and leaves the bodies nameless. I can't stop wondering what it would feel like to arouse relation at the place of its derealization, inside his "gastric mucosa, arranged in the usual rugal folds and unremarkable," or beside "the underlying renal cortices, sharply delineated from the medullary pyramids, which are purple to tan and unremarkable." My bladder floats in the same somatic void from which his meat's been drawn, quartered and sublimed into a medium where love destroys its object, failing to distinguish opposites, the pleural cavity itself depriving the body of any singularity in excess of the process that has tagged its parts. I don't mean severe facial trauma and right leg amputation, nor lower-left leg fracture and pulmonary embolism, nor left leg prosthesis and shrapnel lesion, but the reported appearance of his "unremarkable genitalia," extraordinarily rendered. Which gets me thinking about my first fuck, a boy named Andy, to whose personal ad I desperately responded in the Amherst Valley Voice with a hand-written letter in 1984 after years of interminable fantasy failed to materialize the flesh I craved, and whose genitals were anything but unremarkable. Note how my reference to handwriting forges a link between the autopsy report and my memory of doing it with Andy in the woods on my dad's camp blanket, which may have been army-issued back in the forties, and which I'd grown accustomed to keeping in the car just in case, though I can't tell you what I was thinking, I mean, it was dark, and the trees at the foot of that modest peak on the edge of town were thick, so the link between a detainee's organ function and my lousy arousal was already there, haunting psychic backwash, just waiting to be triggered. This is all very fresh, but I can't remember when I first imagined my body being pummeled by a soldier's dirty slab, the feeding tube being of more recent provenance, like the formless drape over the abyss his legs create, or an abscess in meat processed at the U.S. base just outside Kabul. Food, being the materialization of this estrangement, the thing about the old days, well, "they the old days," and while new rules allow photographs of casualties, the prohibition on recognizable faces and other identifiable features persists, ostensibly to protect the family. What I finally want to confess is that I've failed the promise of the poem to come upon him properly, the hoary "house of being," another name for market stress, or house arrest, or whatever binds me to the particulate matter of causal force, bone-dust. As Blake would have it, the elect can't be redeemed from heaps of smoking rubble, a blank in nature money rushes in to fill, but I'm still trying to sense the feeling of this form. I've even learned to respond to the need by heart and feel myself reaching for a friend, these scenes of recent enclosure, my detainee's body being the hazardous substrate of all the stuff we don't produce but upon which the dream of our wellbeing hangs, a gift from nowhere, like darkness in its purest form when even the light itself is dark. Or, as Brenda would have it, when the person's been absorbed by the body, identity fails its self-possession. But even this fails to penetrate my psycho-geography, the entire coastline, militarized for a transit corridor, water from Anatolia, water from Mesopotamia, it all ends up in L.A.. In other words, being *is* money, the conjunctive link of each relation thrown under the big wheel of ontology, which is my way of getting the sun into every line of verse, the fact that you can't see the goods being the only proof they exist. Possibility itself, like systemic risk, the caption beneath the photo reads "member of U.S. kill team poses behind dead body" resulting in my own evasion, this persistent failure to mourn, fodder for interminable sadness. As for the things that embarrass me most, I never turn down a free sample and my fantasies involve being fucked by day laborers, though these are arbitrary placeholders, little stages I trot out on occasion for performance enhanced tricks, no substitute for the thing I've been dying to tell you but still can't fathom. What will it take to arrive at so impossible an event, to lend positive content to the scene of that blank, a fossil of the future already lodged inside my stool. And what other feeling would be the right feeling to have when feeling itself has become obscene, the way open access buries these structural violations under the sign of love which, failing its calling to make something common, opens an empty place [——] for this perversion. I mean, if you have the money, it's easy to privatize yr writing. It always feels good to feel wanted, like selling real estate with the hope that there will be someone to connect with inside the house. I'm just trying to be realistic without being naïve, so I go on touring the site, moving thru forests of unsingable delights, the trees along the perimeter expanding with the earth, while all my men get stoned on disbelief. This yields the system's waste, the only universal being the site of a redacted name, whatever refuses proper integration, anticipatory omen of a common place thus far only rumored.

HOCUS–POCUS(1)

'Hocus-pocus" is said to be a monkish muddle for "Hoc est corpus" (the formula, "This is the body [of Christ]," etc.), a corruption of fantastic origin. And if it be true that the ignorant and juggling priests who gabble Latin which they do not understand, instead of saying "Hoc est corpus" transformed it into "hocus-pocus," may we not legitimately form the word "hoax" from this?

William Swinton
Rambles Among Words (1859)

OF ATTRACTIVE BODIES
OR, EVIDENCE OF INJURY

I dare not defile the likes of you, he writes, nor the likes of the parts of you, for I believe that the likes of you and the parts of you stand or fall with my poems, and that they are my poems. Head, neck, hair, ears, drop and tympan of the ears. Eyes, yes, eye-fringes, iris of the eye, eye-brows, and the waking or sleeping of the lids. Mouth, tongue, lips, teeth, roof of the mouth, jaws, and the jaw-hinges. Endotracheal tube, central venous line. Multiple intravenous puncture sites on right arm and antecubital fossa. Cheeks, temples, forehead, chin, throat, back of the neck, neck-slue. Nose, nostrils of the nose, and the partition. Bilateral adhesions noted in both pleural cavities. External automatic defibrillator pads on chest. Strong shoulders, manly beard, scapula, hind-shoulders, and the ample side-round of the chest. Upper-arm, arm-pit, elbow-socket, lower-arm, arm-sinews, arm-bones. All body organs in the normal anatomical position. Subcutaneous fat layer of the abdominal wall (unremarkable). The brain in its folds inside the skull-frame. Heart-valves, palate-valves, the sex. Dura mater and falx cerebri (intact). Leptomeninges (thin and delicate), cerebral hemispheres (symmetrical), the structures at the base of the brain, cranial nerves and vessels (no evidence of trauma). Neck, hyoid bone and thyroid cartilege (intact). Wrist and wrist-joints, hand, palm, knuckles, thumb, fore-finger, finger-balls, finger-joints, finger-nails. Broad breast-front, curling hair of the breast, breast-bone, breast-side. Ribs, belly, back-bone, joints of the back-bone. Heart (280 grams), pericardial surfaces (smooth, glistening and unremarkable), pericardial sac (free of significant fluid and adhesions). Epicardium (smooth and unremarkable), myocardium (red-brown, firm and grossly unremarkable), aorta and major branches, venae cavae and their major tributaries. Leg-fibres, knee, knee-pan, upper-leg, under leg. Ankles, instep, foot-ball, toes, toe-joints, the heel. All attitudes, all the shapeliness, all the belongings of yr body, or of any one's body. All sympathies, tears, laughter, weeping, love-looks, love-perturbations and risings. The voice, articulation, language, whispering, shouting aloud. The lung-sponges, the stomach-sac, the bowels sweet and clean. Lungs (right and left, 650 grams and 600 grams respectively), upper airway of the respiratory system (clear of debris and foreign material), the mucosal surfaces (smooth, yellow-tan and unremarkable), pleural surfaces, pulmonary parenchyma (red-purple and exuding a moderate amount of body fluid with no focal lesions identified), the pulmonary arteries (normally developed, patent and without thrombus or embolus). Liver and biliary system (1300 grams), hepatic capsule (smooth, glistening and intact, covering dark red-brown, moderately congested parenchyma with no focal lesions notes), gallbladder (contains green-brown, mucoid bile), musoca (velvety and unremarkable), extrahepatic tree (patent, without evidence of calculi). Alimentary tract, esophagus (lined by gray-white mucosa), gastric mucosa (arranged in usual rugal folds and unremarkable), stomach (distended with partially digested food with no evidence of mucosal or vascular injury), small and large bowels (unremarkable), pancreas (normal pink-tan lobulated appearance and patent ducts), appendix (present and unremarkable). Hips, hip-sockets, hip-strength, inward and outward round, man-balls, man-root. Strong set of thighs, well carrying the trunk above. External genitalia (circumcised adult male with bilaterally descended and unremarkable testes). Genitourinary system, renal capsules (smooth and thin, semi-transparent), underlying smooth, red-brown cortical surfaces, cortices sharply delineated from the medullary pyramids (red-purple to tan and unremarkable), calyces, pelves and ureters (unremarkable), urinary bladder (unremarkable with clear yellow urine), right and left kidney (100 grams each). Pulse, digestion, sweat, sleep, walking, swimming. Poise on the hips, leaping, reclining, embracing, arm-curving and tightening. The continual changes of the flex of the mouth and around the eyes. The skin, the sun-burnt shade, freckles, hair. The curious sympathy one feels, when feeling with the hand the naked meat of the body. The reticuloendothelial system, the spleen (120 grams, smooth, intact capsule, red-purple and moderately firm parenchyma), the lymphoid follicles (unremarkable), the regional lymph nodes (normal in appearance). The endocrine system, pituitary, thyroid and adrenal glands (all unremarkable). Musculoskeletal system (normal, with no bone or joint abnormalities). The circling rivers, the breath, and breathing it in and out. The beauty of the waist, the hips, and thence downward toward the knees. All the thin red jellies within you, or within me, the bones, and the marrow in the bones. A healed fractured right humerus. Representative sections of the major organs (retained in formalin). Muscle development (normal). Specimens retained for toxicological and DNA identification: blood (heart), vitreous fluid, bile, urine, stomach contents, tissue samples from liver, lung, kidney, spleen, brain, psoas and adipose tissue.

FALSE COMMUNIQUÉ

And so I sing this body on a table
For since the war I've read reports i
- magined events studied pro

- cedures assisting incarceration
W/ coroners who must know
Something and whose language

Rushes like unfettered streams on
- ly half-knowing the work I mean
Check out this wonder of a guy

A spectacle withdrawn & covered
With my latinate phrases issue
Displace so gorgeous a figure again

- st a ground of organs & viscera
For which the world moves its
Product making nothing this body

Linking it to that body my body
Severed from animal & plant over
Which production cycles steadily

Roll whose head the all-baffling
Brain eviscerates evacuates exa
- mines limbs jaundiced brown a

Cunning tendon nerve now strip
- ped so you still can't see things
But just imagine his dreamy eyes

Deadened plucked volition flakes
Inside pleural cavities mere sacs
Upon a table grey-white smooth

Mucosa distended stomach not
Flabby good-sized arms legs
Ureters & genitalia unremarkable

Interior what dura mater drapes
And mysteries haunt the clear
Yellow urine the pericardial bag

From which his prick might other
- wise rise normally with blood no
Longer running red runs to brown

Purple to tan as swelling jets pass
- ions patient swollen one would
Think not there since invisible

Condemned inside his fat the start
Of revolutions durable matter
Is thin delicate yielding countless

Embodiments baffling republics
Whose cranial nerves contest
My enjoyments will arrive

From the offspring of his offspring
Thru our bleakest time I come

— from him myself.

FALSE COMMUNIQUÉ

One civilian detainee was found
Unresponsive with a ligature
Or plastic band around my cock

A bottle ring pops pigeon death
In cell behavior health unit joint
Task force Guantanamo 2200 hours

When the ligature gets cut I come
Without remorse on the source
Of light his electric body being

Banished to mulch organic comp
- osition capital dividing luminous
Flux a rumor a burden of labor

Having fallen away from the tend
- ency of profit to rise and fall w/
The quality of radiance his cock

The way any man will use my hands
Like vitreous fluid his urine emits
So diffused a glow no needle-like

Beam thru pores of junk no evi
- dence of trauma resuscitation
Efforts begging immediate organ

- ization to turn blood back
To military cargo my skin
Now shares

> *— with a tank.*

FALSE COMMUNIQUÉ

And as if to discredit all protest
- ant thought as ephemeral med
- ical treatment facility efforts fail

To revive [——] dead at 2300
Hours records reveal a ligature
Another absent cause whose

Effects themselves withdraw into
The fine textures of a detainee
- 's cauterized wounds whose emp

- tied bowels divide my poem's time
Between luminous flux & corporeal
Mass measured rate of increase where

- by the words surface expand & bloat
His body being a quandary or tension
Can reveal the nature of value being

Anti-social personality stressors
Confinement history of suicidal idea
- tion gestures & multiple failed

Attempts hunger involuntarily fed
And escorted in single point leg
Shackled w/ mask over mouth it

Keeps him from spitting biting
Swallowing the tongue liquidates
Whatever totality his dead body

Confirms the thing

— my pleasure negates.

FALSE COMMUNIQUÉ

The poem opens what space
Deprives sentience turns to dry cell
Water put off during observation

Case under investigation by naval
Criminal authority for autopsy
Armed forces medical examiner

Under IAW title 10 U.S. code 1471
Subject identified by visual recog
- nition looks nothing like what I

See when I see anything at all who
- se ID tags & fingerprints tissue
Samples obtained for DNA equals

Asphyxia due to ligature death
Being a ring around my cock stran
- gulation suicide by something

Used for tying when I come join
- ing letters the decedent could be
Viewed thru cell window not

Breathing on my floor in fetal
Position his right side covered
With blanket & both feet exposed

        — to my forced production of meaning.

FALSE COMMUNIQUÉ

As for clothing plastic flex
- i cuffs brown bags around
His hands being a domain

Of clear visibility submitted
To my agents attending auto
- psy's happy gaze each organ

A refuge expelled desire his
Punishment makes a me
- mory of me these holes a

Great clarity trembles a feel
- ing that precedes my body
Well equipped w/ distance

Between his corpse & what
Privacy I court whose fate
Contains crushed residues

Of everything properly mine
The density this double silence
Natural history demands

A ligature identical to one el
- astic band an intact pair
White briefs matching those

Said to have been issued to
Decedent & retained being
What it means to be in rel

- ation to a domain of events
Colors variations tiny anoma
- lies receptive to my deviant

Appeal made inside his body
As if an organ were being
Caressed by an elegant hand

With no prior language one
Pathological fact measures
The space between my body

And this thing most deeply
Shared

　　　　　　　— our happiness impossible to name.

HOCUS–POCUS(2)

CAVITIES OF LIGHT

His body like a slab of light bursts into this field of white. Now it's cooling down as my thoughts about him find their heat. The skin expels strange radiance *this blank wherein my writing hovers* makes my tongue enlarge and my face break out, each organ yielding noisome fluid. Metal salts condense in the blood and amplify intensity. I need to believe this sentence follows the existence of something, a plosive hum or drone, an object in my head, whatever cuts on facial planes. Under grave prismatic glare, the tissue peels away, passing daily with my urine. The intestines shed internal slough, and we see it pass thru his rectum. Dead light emanates from such vague humors, concealing intravenous holes on his right arm and antecubital fossa. Such light is thrown upon my cornea, as the image stretches to inconceivable peripheries equal only to the surface area of rentable space where the appearance of military cargo becomes my own veil of particles. Subcutaneous fat cushions the emanation of even fainter waves, while the garbage that his organs make sublimes into profit, each marketable product sharing something of value with that tank. The arterial trachea, esophagus and tongue peel away in turn, as the body rejects each membranous surface, like a memory of home and the first bed I came in. What language overcomes the distance between this visionary space and the rational zone of the coroner's report to which his body's destined. His piss emits the same radiant glow, the way a pond in Thoreau's *Maine Woods* might glow, dividing luminous flux from the body's planar surface. For a moment I take his open skin for the source of my sentence. Serial sectioning of the brain reveals yet another scene of brilliance, as both stem and cerebellum emerge from the body in candescent gowns. On first sight, his light suggests a quality known to enhance the satisfaction of office employees, while allowing cannabis to grow strong and healthy, the same light needed for breeding poultry. His body's predicament, being just as rational, like the albuminous skin of an egg, erects its figure anterior to every gaze. Upon further sectioning, the cerebral hemisphere lets go a bulb of fire in a muted haze that dampens the atmosphere around this resting surface. A veneer of carbon waste, how it slumbers in my speech, the way his body dreams me here. The gurney no longer exists on solid ground, his body being an improper sexual object for which I ought to be sentenced. And so a meaning hangs over us, the structure of corporeal space, a crack between what we can perceive and what we can say. I make a little souvenir of hair and teeth glowing with residual heat, turning my pocket into a reliquary, my fantasy, his mausoleum. The body is thus secured inside a bean-sized hole, his limbs taxonomized, his face covered with luminous sores betraying every smooth pricing surface, a constellation of lesions through which the light moves in patterns that allow me to read the report. Plasma scrims through pores of junk, a beautiful pyrotechnic sun, a spasm of glass exploding from his skull. A needle-like beam protrudes through the epidermal tissue, and even wider bands transport the dura mater, each organ arrayed, bearing some concealed relation, now mechanically rendered visible. His penis, semi-erect, a feather of light now touching me gently. Cranial nerves spawn white arcs of joy, each of which perplexes, but whose quandary reveals true radiance, no evidence of trauma. A haptic rose, my dead giveaway. As always, the scandal is hushed in deep reserves of light. The secret of his sacred beam's no secret, but absolute exposure to rule, whose measures my darkness defies. Anyone who has looked directly at the source knows that this is only true.

THE LIGATURE

Looking sadly at my cock, I begin rereading the autopsy report. "A civilian detainee was found unresponsive in his cell with a ligature." With no referent for what that word "ligature" might denote, I imagine the metal clasp for securing a musical reed, like the dented one on my first clarinet, a thing with which I conducted my earliest experiments in masturbation, before the leather cord, the plastic cuff and clamp. I'm aroused by the suggestion of his body lying prone and feel myself getting hard, the way the structure of this sentence hardens around his figure, or the way a ligature disrupts the flow of oxygen to the dura mater, stimulating cell tissue due to a lack of endorphins, a deficit that has my pleasure centers craving. Upon being raised, his forehead reveals a cluster of dark lesions in which I can see my face breakout in the mirror. His gaze falls on my flaccid prick *evidence of injury* false promise of love moving thru thick undergrowth of ligament and sinew, suggesting a thicket of leaves and wood. As my hand searches for a thigh inside the pocket, a ligature becomes a thing of pleasure, like the plastic band of his institutional briefs, which I imagine removing with my teeth. Nothing requires more patience than the shadow of this thing pressing from above the bed. Hovering, a halo, the word "ligature" assumes the importance of a punctum, contracting aura, at once instrument and vehicle of our transport. Were this elastic cord to be seen in some other light, it might be stretched along an empty horizon, coding as paradise, improving conditions of the general seizure. Like a musical slur, this surgical thread binds my letters. When lifted, his scrotum reveals my ligature's scar for photographs and documentation under enhanced illumination. This is how his punishment makes a memory of me, while the ligature links his body, at its most radically specific point, to the common good and its negation. And so, the individual case becomes one with universal interest, binding body & situation. For contrast, there's debridement, a surgical removal of dead tissue from a wound, where I still recall being fucked by my soldier before he pulls out in accord with a set of conventions, which, like grammar, govern the relations between subjects and objects within normal frames of reference, binding everything in advance to a deferred period, like my detainee's corpse, the brightest moment in our repertoire of truth. His "unremarkable genitalia" denoted in the report hint at the girth of a complementary hole, which reveals itself in the ligature's light as I kneel before him on the table. Serial incisions show no evidence of injury, as if his testicles had been shorn, served up in a deep ragout to compensate for hemorrhaged accounts, a cavity emptied of dura mater and replaced with my cum, which I collect in advance for very hygienic purposes, my poem, still wired to the logic of future attacks. Peeled away, the skin reveals the extent of the ligature's reach, another absent cause, whose effects are themselves withdrawn into the fine textures of my detainee's cauterized sores. This truth no doubt follows the existence of something, a hill a cell a wood a limb, or the words for these things, which might themselves stand for nothing, a hole in militarized common sense, a body that repels every pronoun, open to the whole fucking assembly before which I tremble, naked and pathetic. I think you may be ready to enter the garden, he says. That's when I drive my tongue inside, like the general public anxious to see his balls snipped off with a pair of scissors, or his whole body disemboweled with a hot iron poker, or even more refined instruments issued by my corps of engineers. So I place the cord around his cock while looking sadly at my own, establishing equivalence between organs and garbage. He claims to be much older, without having achieved a single orgasm in his twelve years behind bars. Yr body, my devotional kink, what do I mean when I say "I burn with love for you'? I'm still seeking a lyric structure that might allow me to ask this question, a sentence feeling for its own conditions but whose words continue to elude them, for example, "On my knees, in the back of the cell, he holds my head to the rim of his latrine, just close enough for me to smell the crap he left there only an hour ago, and this fantasy turns me on to such a degree that I can feel a tiny bead of cum on the head of my dick, though I'm not even hard, as if whatever I'm breathing from that metal expanse might coincide with the limit of our episteme and the whole taxonomy of signs that make our life world visible at the expense of what can not appear here." But I don't want this sentence to be an example of anything. Once his body is admitted and a relation felt, narrative returns like the repressed, which had been there all along, spilling over the structure of my sentence, awaiting its own improper content. Plastic flexi-cuffs around his hands and a ligature said to be identical to the elastic band of his army-issued briefs, neutered on contact with my syntax, turning that part of him that has no name, the part to which my happiness clings, into the most fungible of things, his "unremarkable genitalia." Still, I can run my tongue along their edge, forcing arousal while reading this report where the wrongness of my object-choice feels unavoidable, like the limit of our knowledge as radical particularity becomes the hoax upon which the falseness of the universal hangs. Prone to auto-fellate, he achieves satisfaction without the assistance of this idea, but the ligature intensifies the pleasure of release as its tightening rigs the precarity of my own position, a body susceptible to change and unready to die. So I submit to what I can't master and spread my legs for his dreamy cock, remarkable for its perfect nest of shiny black hairs. There will always be someone who falls outside the general equality, being unimaginable from inside the frame. Take me on all fours, for example, his dick, being the most civic of fountains when he pisses on my face, a global rite, running like an alpine stream in Wordsworth's *Prelude*. This makes the rupture visceral, like the purity of law whose victorious force polices our difference, now spreading with his penile girth, the heavy weight of a stallion's balls, diminished with his discharge, the total body being but an effect of its perceived effects. And so, I hollow out a cunt in his corpse *my opening to the other* and fuck a patient orifice. This is how my love, in order to be love, is enflamed and extinguished in the language of his "unremarkable genitalia." Addressing the flesh with serial sectioning and still no evidence of trauma, I rub him down with alcohol and ignite the body, tightening the cord upon discharge, making further examination unnecessary.

A NOTE ON THESE PROCEEDINGS

This is what it takes to sense the insensate, making a common place palpable in the fabricated delights of his body. The more withdrawn my detainee, the more strenuously the sentence *my sensation delivery system* pushes against the social crust that bans relation here where it's most intense. As flesh inclines toward flesh, there's inconsolable grief in the arousal of unknown pleasures. What's most unspeakable about his body converges with what's most banal *a common place that sings thru everything* as the false fluency of his autopsied corpse disappears in an endless flow of readymade phrases, weird ether of forgotten dismemberments. The report preserves a trace of them *hardened & alienated* so withdrawn that it requires this unfathomable reach to span an otherwise unbridgeable gulf, the amplification of pleasure's signs being the means by which to perceive an occulted bond. Larger than the imaginary whole from which it's been excluded, his body shifts our common measure, a mystery with no code to crack. What word isn't obscene under such conditions? This is how a detainee makes himself felt inside a sentence that will never contain him, an absence whose enormity is otherwise inconceivable beyond this rhetorical extravagance, acme of sentiment and kitsch. His interminable internment needs the secret labor of my entire body. This last proposition can't be true, but if love's realization implies a revolution in the very structure of our life-world signaling the end of a truth whose universality *forever false* hangs on the death of every particular, then his body demands a love I can barely even intimate.

FLASHBACK

In early 2000, my detainee was handed a cassette tape containing a message from the now deceased Shaykh discussing jihad. He soon traveled by bus to Quetta PK where he stayed with several hundred others at a Taliban safe house before going by taxi to Kabul. From there, several trucks transported him to the gathering center in the Khwaja Ghar area near a river close to the border of Tajikistan, approximately eight kilometers behind the front lines. He already knew how to operate an AK-47 and handle grenades from when he was a youth in Yemen. From the gathering center, two thousand or more people were distributed to various points nearby. While there, he heard on the radio about the 11 September 2001 attacks, which he noted were wrong because Islam does not permit the killing of innocent people. Shortly thereafter, Northern Alliance forces increased the intensity of operations, and aerial bombings concentrated on the Khwaja Ghar area. My detainee estimated that 1,300 people were killed as a result of the bombings. Then he departed from Kunduz around the 9th day of Ramadan 2001 and was present at the uprising at Qala-i-Jangi, where he was wounded during the initial stages. His right abdomen was grazed and he was shot in the left hand. The round went through his hand and exited the palm and he lay bleeding in the center of the courtyard for about twenty hours, after which he walked into a basement and remained there for the duration of the uprising. Northern Alliance troops fired rockets into the basement in order to drive combatants out. The basement was then flooded with water resulting in the drowning of several people. At around the seventh day, my detainee was ordered to surrender and moved to Sheberghan, AF by truck where he spent four days in the prison and was treated for his wounds before being transferred to U.S. custody at the Kandahar Detention Facility.

IDENTIFICATION OF THE BODY

And so living nite dissipates in the brightness of death. A lum
- inous moment in our repertoire of truth, his body perjured
As the sun. Reconstitution of his organs presses thru
The scrim of an eye, maps my body's functions to a state
Of cold resolve, this plenum of sensation, skin of the world.

His skin draws me back to a scene of plenty, something
That the mind made, but is not the mind, false Eden
Of a common world. There was no shortage of corpses
Back then, no need to rob graves or perform anatomical
Black masses, the public square having already been stationed

In the blinding light of autopsy, a white visibility, a shrouded
Brown charade. In the beginning, the conflict wasn't between
The rising tides of East and West nor some youthful ideology
Pressed against old beliefs, but incompatible forms of know
- how, one proceeding from the eye, the other from words.

Mine eye having been jellied, my words derive from his
Remains and share nothing with his corpse though identical
In all their mediations, my poem like a report from beyond
The shadows, his originating spark, confusing swollen
Tongues, persistent tremors and corresponding lesions.

My problem hangs inside vast networks of waste, systems
Fantasies involving his gentle fist, whereby conjugated
Muscle might one day yield the pleasures of non-production.
So long as a promise of variation, deviation, and anomaly
Holds sway, his tissuey surface usurps my screen, displacing

The alimentary canal, relieving my desire to come deep inside
His intestinal tract, or he inside mine eye already fattened
With the abuse these words incite, an imagined unity, vast waves
Dispersing the body's meanings across a white field where
His prostate speaks of strike location before incineration.

Death is thus absorbed by the luminous flow or opaque
Mass in which small cysts lay hidden with my signs (they too
Seek transmission) the way the social logic of part & whole
Works itself into the heart whose condition ossifies in flesh
- y columns having already converted into hard & bony tubes

Connecting me to his life just as my car's connected to a ship
- ping lane and the transport of vegetables over seas & borders.
But the general idea of his body bears resemblance to every
Thing, the disease now visible in aneurismal sacs these heavy
Pouches whose interior fills with layers of coagulated sediment

Deposits, a whole archeology of ballistics codified in manuals
And brochures. All this unifies in code traversing organs
Battening the system with military screws made in China fast
- ened to the heart-wall whose rupture produces sudden
Tics in my verse, faults according to the standard operating

Segments of perception as transposed into speech. See how
My lines remain faithful to him like a study of morbid anatomy
The way they envelop, divide and compose his person liquid
- ated in the spongy stuff we've made, and whose identity hangs
On my ability to interpret his fundament being the presence

Of a false passage just inside the rectum where my tongue
Applies its balm. Prior to this moment, the viewfinder pro
- duces only abstract symptoms, a dreamlike vista surrounding
The camp where all these vectors of force collide, extract
- ing transitional carbon-based fuels from shale, or surplus

Value from whatever labor's necessary to pass a fuck
- ing stone thru the tiny slit at one end of his bowel
Just large enough for anything to slip thru thus signaling
Completion of production cycle in his body, so many
Seemingly unrelated phenomena inflaming sensuous

Membranes, the way my house glows like his U.S. Army
- issued briefs, which conceal a whitish shroud that clings
To the subject's tissues and whose band becomes a ligature
Whereby a whole system of communication resolves itself
In a period, or a scene of equal scarcity where pleasure fails

> *— and rages in his absent core.*

FUNERAL RITES

This is how the body of a soldier harbors my love for a detainee. The same river pours over the one without a drop of that love being subtracted from the other. You can see I'm aiming to preserve and nourish both young men under the double ray of tenderness and compassion, but these figures are one and the same, and while my yearning drowns his withdrawn form, my need to feel him close overwhelms the body's inaccessibility, giving way to an equal and opposite excess. Watching him there in his cell *gross misshapen lump* I can't shake the image of a soldier wearing flesh-colored stockings and a wild pink dress. Writing this helps me make sense of what it all means, but how will my song achieve real weight when the closer I get to this feeling *conflict of sensations without a name* the better my chance of arriving at something so general as to pass for money. The promise of a common place hangs on his body [——] appearing now in the tarnished surface of a surveillance lens which becomes my inmost eye. My feelings move here according to a logic at once intimate (recessed & private) and social (exposed & public), the difference merely semantic now realized in his flesh. In the depth of suffering there can be no depravity, so I arouse the pain his death has caused me while conceding the fact that his death has caused me no pain at all. This alone is enough to make me fear for the integrity of my emotional life, as if my fantasy of being fucked by a Gitmo detainee might resurrect his singularity in a park or square where I'm not yet prepared to greet him, where men used to fuck publicly before Grindr and my communards more recently hunkered down to camp. What I really want now, however, is to feel his velvety mucosa as though it were a plush knitted cotton like velour. This is how the sensitivity of his pulmonary cavity responds to heat, turning the impenetrability of an autopsy report toward intelligible joy, its violence, a conjugal bower. Having escaped the warp of productive time, his body courts contrary identities whose fate upon the table bears the trace of everything improperly mine, the stuff of immortality, a portal to paradise, this anatomical dispersion being all that flesh achieves. The clinical gaze mirrors my own, a metallic beam on which my detainee rises together with the body of a military man as their forms converge at once other and the same. Imagining my head in his lap, I'm convinced that my penis is being devoured by fish as though it were bait, a feeling matched in intensity only by a vision of friendship, defying the harness that binds the body to socially useful ends now superseded by his liquidated person. So I close my eyes and consider his Army issued briefs, an image I fill with the weight of his cock swollen with desire for our wellbeing. The idea of my tongue running the length of his spine, then teasing the arch of his foot, makes me quiver. Here in the shadow cast by his cancelled form an even heavier fragrance envelops me as the glands between my thighs work intensely, generating all the familiar symptoms my Propranolol otherwise subdues, exasperating sweat, swollen tongue & quickened pulse. Even my perineum feels enlarged with his body just lying there dreaming me in compromising positions. I want to celebrate utter uselessness with his scrotum in my mouth. But if I so much as stir, the acrid odor inside my bowels escapes, drawing immediate attention to my otherwise inconspicuous form here in the library corner where I'm writing this passage undercover with my hand around my cock concealed inside the pocket whose lining I've conveniently torn. Uttering his name in solitude accomplishes nothing, so I transcribe the words of his autopsy report while reading them aloud as if to cast a spell that will revive some residual feeling in the negative space of his body. Compassion is born in just such a space, says Camille. Like the report itself, I think, where identity is realized in the annihilation of its subject. But the stylization of his body's poses creates a series of persistent gestures that animate my form *head thrown back like Hecuba mourning on the beach* each of which works like a screen to deflect precisely the meanings it appears most to resemble, or a mirror behind which value withdraws, unavailable for use. With torso bent forward, well-built though emaciated, his flesh fills my frame as though a slight change in pressure sucked it all thru an orifice *this fault in my syntax* whose limit limns a ligature when there's no hope for healing or becoming someone else, a fantasy wherein I raise my head to the level of his knees and in supplication beg for his prick before wiping his forehead so drenched with sweat, the disfigured face relieved by darkness out of which his two black eyes go shining. That's when I defy the systematic liquidation of his body simply by asking him what he likes. Nuts and melon, fast cars and pretty views, he says as I service him with my tongue, which reveals a bit of the same rectal mucus noted in the report whereby he achieves identity. Laboring over this glowing wreck, his wasted ass, I taste the hair once cushioning the genitalia, now caught between my teeth and gums. That's when this image appears, harmonious composition of a secret labor, involving the whole of my organization whose indiscriminate passion for waste secretes a lubricant for the general machinery, harnessing the organism at its most vulnerable points, his capillaries, like coral canals, opening onto a vermillion sea. Our only peril being not in death but in love, the singularity of this grief equals the singularity of unknown pleasures, which is nothing singular at all. So I drive my tongue down deeper still. Enthralled by the foul smell, I bring back much to my tongue's delight a bit of shit that had formed around his rectum, so much sweat and curly vapors, the inmost flesh, a dusty fossil. A shudder runs down my spine and I feel in each of my organs the unremarkable denotation of his, each reported humor linked to its complement inside my frame if only by the threads of clinical language, each sentence drawing my body into the vacuous space of that report where new feeling is born in the comingling of common names. What does it mean to love these young men, their theory and their pageantry, whose claims for transcendence find their meaning resolved in stately text. Unlike mine, his life has the shape of his body, though I'm certain that a time will come when the language drawn from him will diminish my abstract core, a literal life whose opaque meaning equals exactly what words say. And again I ask, why is this not my shit, my blood, my sperm. How stupid to say that I recognize his pain when even recognition of the body is impossible. With my eyes shut, the words just spin, the liveliest parts reduced to data like his remarkable cock, the simplicity of a crystal tool taking possession of my mouth, competing only with the spiritual rod of my militiaman. It's cold to my lips, at least in my head, so I postpone the realization of any pleasure, holding back my orgasm *I always come to soon* as if he'd been flayed or quartered, and I cling all the more to this mutilated form or the language that stands in for it, a luminous fog rising high above my bed. As transcription gives way to the need for touch, conditions destroy its possibility and I no longer sense his presence in my lower extremities, indeed I no longer feel anything at all except this burnt desire smoldering inside some withdrawn organ that blocks the sensation it attracts. All this being for the disenchantment of yr enchanted cell.

OPINION

By the time these events find their representation in my poems, my detainee has become a recessed shadow, a vague thread of residual light thrown upon a bell curve, sublimate of breath, a moist decay consumed by molecule and dust, a source of rumor, all glassy surface and smooth economy. His limp prick, an appendage whose metallic lisp lies still on the table, bends, a tiny scar along my side, small enough to go unnoticed. He keeps me open to auto-affection. If only I could feel his hand caressing my thigh, grazing my cock, which begins to harden even now as it chafes against my denim, requiring ointments and powders, rerouting the offense to other sectors where it manifests as outbreak and mercurial stain. It's only the feel of my beating heart I want to give him as he backs me into a corner, takes me from behind and I open without condition imagining his hand up my ass, gentle at the fundament, forearm engulfed by cavity, approaching the source of rhythm which, as Bob notes, is just past "the trap" in the intestines, where nothing but a filmy tissue separates one's hand from the beloved's heart. During the whole of this episode, I can't stop thinking about that canal full of cows, a whole generation of dying beef, a bad infinity whose colliding forces sink beneath my poem's shiny coat and percolate, as if we could only know things insofar as we know their names, these bubbles that rise in my mouth as I read, all valorized gas, his body, my perjured commons.

CONTRIBUTION TO A CRITIQUE
OF MY PHILOSOPHY OF ARDOR

Love requires more of me the way his body wastes
In radical chains it won't be emancipated w/o some
- thing like revolution for which my poems offer no

- thing more than a paltry sign a peculiar quality like his
Suffering it has universal character and can't be redressed
B/c the violence done to it is not particular but violence

In general at once common & exceptional so the effort
To demilitarize my desire must bear generic implication
For the poem finally to be "the individual expression

Of our universal experience" I mean human & abstract
But these propositions are false the way any p. o. v.
That privileges the universal *human rights* can only be

False tho I still want to love him in a way that's not
I mean I want to impute for all the choice of one
The object of my affection being not "my" object but yrs

Ours the aura of his briefs sharing qualities w/ a fable
- d first kiss amplified subjectivity this fantasy bound
Right here at the base of my balls where it pressures

The prostate & makes me come touching objective
Conditions I mean the structure of automatic deposits
Each mediates my relation to someone's liquid

- ated personhood the way my love materializes in a body
The universal can't acknowledge w/o destroying itself
Free of subjective spells my love overcomes idealist ass

- umptions that its precious thing exists only for me the part
- icularity of my perverted choice being too banal & poetic
His figure's vacant gulf whose secret resolves itself

In moist lubrication the promise of a feeling

— irreducible to money.

OPEN UP A FEW CORPSES

What we find when opening up the body can't be detached from the regimen, diet and waste of my detainee's everyday life. Characterized by diurnal meditation & prayers resembling sleep, his renal capsules appear to be smooth. Everything else is transparent and peels with ease. This requires no poetry, tho the cause of death can't be traced to any one stimulus without recourse to strange figures. Whatever triggers the cessation of life does not belong to the light of day, so the body becomes a terminus, a grammatical period from whose localization a whole history can be retrojected into space, offered up like a testament to some anterior truth whose final cause coincides with its conditions, back-feeding sense into unrelated events, encounters & disjointed signs, all of which now appear meaningful. After graduation, for example, the deceased worked for his father on the family farm in Yemen where they raised livestock and grew watermelons, tomatoes and corn. Unlike such fruits, his valves are stained with dark red plumes. This condition of the heart involves the whole social organism, tho it may be confined to one or more portions of the septum, like the ventricles whose fleshy columns are covered in a viscid white jelly. This is how the structure of his cell floats inside my body, the time of captivity itself, the fiber of this symptomatic swelling. So detention is an autopsy already waiting in the body's darkness, the spontaneous form of a civic consciousness. Anyone who really looks can see that the ligature's effects are not distributed evenly throughout the anatomical mass. This is how an epidermal surface goes from being a structure of the observed to a figure of the onlooker, the way the symptoms themselves migrate thru a space whose economy appears as though it were my own morbid anatomy. Only the most external cells resist, because autopsy anticipates every connection, bursting open the wonders of genesis with the splendid rigors of desiccation, the corpse itself being all that remains of a positive truth, a tumor in the pleural cavity that finds its rhetorical figure embodied in lockdown whereby my detainee becomes the rediscovered portrait of the world that excludes him. His body, a prosthetic of order itself, is the source of a meaning never its own, a dead weight like the material support he provides the total system. In other words, to know the cause is to subtract the body from its conditions, an operation that autopsy theoretically reverses, restoring singularity to the corpus after the fact by virtue of any anomaly whatever. And so the camp distributes his physique thru everything it constitutes, communicating the problem by phone. This is how a detainee's cell penetrates my bedroom. The mechanism works in a way similar to how animal life is extinguished: sensory suppression first, followed by the weakening of locomotion, the rigidity of muscles and diminution of their contractibility, quasi-paralysis of the intestines and, finally, immobilization of the heart. Everything is dirtied *even this vulgarity* creating a contradictory purity *my orgasm* as the precise time of expiration slides along the entire length of confinement. Death thus loses its opacity and becomes the means whereby the whole duration of the offence can be integrated with the mobile space [——] of incarceration itself contained by the same processes that lend autopsy's service to the state. Militarization is thereby perfected by its medicalization, serving the promotion of *homo sanitaire* from whose universal form all necrosis is eliminated, leaving each particular to its living defeat and proper hostility, tho cherished still, the way I cherish you, being the only thing that tells me what I am.

DEMON OF ANALOGY

Now that I've written these things, I'm beginning to realize that my detainee is but one in a series of substitutes for someone else, his body a stand-in for another body lost to me, a loss to which I've clung for years, a death for which I've punished myself *masochism being the price of psychic coherence* as if I could have prevented it had I only known how to love. The excesses of these fantasies *demons of my anal logic* remediate an interminable melancholia *reactionary self-preservation* redressing my failure to overcome a specter of desertion *failure of my poem to save you*. Propositions like these are always shortsighted, falling prey to the morality they abjure. So in order to remove his body from the use to which it's been consigned, I gravitate toward a vanishing point of absolute uselessness where my extravagance finds its equal in trash. His lungs were useless, too, and I'd inject the anti-fungal daily thru a catheter in his back then suck the aspergillus out. Over the years, my narrative has become one of inconsistent repetition, unable to reconcile abandonment and care. He was gentle with leather, I once wrote, and he'd bind my cock and cradle my sleep before I fled our little *balcon* to old hotels in Cairo. You were sick and needed me, or at least I've grown accustomed to telling myself, but there's always another narrative, a truer one, our friend Mary would say, whose conventions might make me suffer less. Now I string together random phrases he left in the margins of books, my ear to the ouija. For example, if the good life depends on the exclusion of a detainee's unremarkable organs, let's stimulate a pleasure commensurable to that ethical violence and imagine community where it's been rendered impossible, a concession to social media where the body disappears behind a proper name, point of intensity in a heaven of stars, like the wound in his back, I think, where the tube goes in and anticipates another hole, the common place a body dreams, or rather its obstruction. So the idea's come from you all along, another platitude like his unspeakable genitalia, forensic effect of enclosure, this most disfluent thing, evisceration of the ear. Condemned as waste, his body becomes our shared resource returned to profane use, my devotional kink. What's it take for so objective a void to find its subjective equivalent? It's all in your head love, he whispers and laughs at my therapeutic literature. But whatever confidence I have in being connected to him still thru the fabled cavity of light can promise only phantasms. That's when I close my eyes and pretend to see the danger as if the crisis were my inner life, an imaginary solution to real contradictions, the way ideology becomes the effluvia of my senses, an order unable to smell its own fundament, this being no solution at all.

A NEW ECONOMY OF BODIES AND PLEASURES

This would be the place in the story where I take him in my mouth again, begging passage to the rectal ducts, extracting his secrets with a curious tongue, prosthetic extension of my gummy self, excess of a body whose grids of sense sanitize an exchange now spilling on command. As his body becomes a casualty of the labor that penetrates it *military hardware, medical needles, enteral tubing* my poems struggle against reason to turn the site of penetration into a scene of shameless pleasure *utopia* if only to make the obstruction to that end perceptible. Still, I wonder whether it's possible "to transmute death, torture, hatred into love, communion, life," as Robbie suggests my poems do, or whether the writing can only materialize the ethical bind that traps this erotic transfer of energy, arousing the affective blocks & psychic clots that keep the body emotionally remote. Imagining his loneliness *nothing like that stupid cloud* I can't advance beyond my own. "This love isn't play anymore and I'm not it personally," writes Notley, a line I recall while wondering whether love for his person requires some impossible consciousness of non-personhood *bad infinity of proper names* suspending every demand that I remain the equal of myself when fucking. Fatty or albuminous, his body may well be a set of conditions with no secrets, but to liberate the word of the report *already autonomous* is not to emancipate its referent. This is how the body provides the material support for representations already gathered, language organized according to a static gaze. The absolute eye cadaverizes the febrile nervure of life turning the exquisite forest of his hair into a tangle of ligaments and sinew as my detainee levitates toward the universality of code. The enumeration of pathological facts—gangrene of the urinary tract or some portion of the bowel, for example, a dark offensive mass limited by a band of highly congested tissues—all this might be said to correspond with a series of astronomical events, a catalog of stamps, or a handbook of exotic tropical fish, each requiring only a few details to lend shape to the individual thing, mere adjunct of its death. Thus his body is withdrawn from perception even as it penetrates my rectum. So it's already been autopsied *dead on arrival* its organs regulated to omit no function, provoking these torsions in my syntax, a new structure of space, anything so as not to hear the word "unremarkable" again. This is how death before dying *we're already dead* throws truth into the shadow of a feeding block divorced from old sympathies and forgotten indignations. His body can't expose itself to the senses but reveals itself to calculated language *my processed core* which the writing will now organize. Left to float along the grey frontier of the visible where everything connects to everything else—my intestinal tract & his enteral nourishment—death no longer looks like something imported from wilderness *the stone, the sky, the moss* nor is any personal item needed to complete its spell, for it's enough that the body be removed from natural functioning to cough up its meaning. In other words, his corpus has already been erotically transfigured and now appears as nature itself. Without my eyes succumbing to this strange mirage, the fatty grey textures found along his organs comprise a dermal surface with no terrestrial parallel, a cellular sheath that can be cut like lard, the way the membrane enveloping the liver can be pulled away without trauma, revealing a mass of small seeds in a tissue bed. This prohibition against physical contact silences the bone beneath our collective experience and its grotesque image on Facebook. So I position myself beside his chair and allow my hand to slip from table to lap where I feel the rising heat in his groin. The space between our limbs has been diminished by cramped quarters and human warmth as the sun turns wisteria into a concentrated aroma, which like a civet meant to allay hints of decay saturates the room and eliminates the more offensive odor rising from the gurney. The first touch being the most frightening, my hand moves to caress his thigh, which I've returned to life by simple spell, as if the force of my sentence were rigged to reverse the temporal might of abomination, his body now inclining toward my palm. His organ, my mouth, so inadequate to sing. But if the body's more than what's contained by skin, I mean, if there's more to the flesh than what's been ceded by code, how can we arouse this excess? Okay, so I do all these things, but the pathetic limpness of my prick, which I'd rather have him sever, has me on my knees, snout poking round the beauty of his glorious hole *deciduous odor of autumn mulch* anything to taste the secret of my social order.

AS FOR MYSELF IN THE PRESENT

Even Bruce notices. We were sharing stories over lunch at the Oyster Bar about the deaths of friends, and one in particular with whom I'd been out of touch for over a decade but whose passing, which I'd only learned about by uncanny occurrence, nonetheless stirred something deep in me as if no loss of intimacy had intervened with the years, and of course Bruce is interested in the precise kind of intimacy we shared so I tell him that, though straight, David desired queerly and we had slept together on several occasions quite tenderly, to which Bruce queries, "Do you think you might write about him?," a question I pass over quickly as if it were inconsequential (why would I do that?, I think) and then I forget about it as the conversation drifts here and there on our walk around the Castro after lunch before arriving back in Bruce's kitchen about an hour later, preparing some tea, eating some chocolate, at which point he picks up the thread of our lunchtime narrations as if they had never been dropped, the way Eric Dolphy might return to a melody after a lengthy improvisation, or the way my grandmother used to return so brilliantly to a theme after an errant series of digressions whose vagaries would argue for an absolute loss of mind, or the way a writer of New Narrative might slip from one story to another within which the first is framed and without which it would be impossible to situate the present of narration, suggesting how no one story can ever hold its own in isolation, requiring a secondary story to contextualize it and a tertiary to which it can't but give rise, and just like that Bruce says, "I've been thinking about how hard it is for you to write about James," whose death twenty years ago continues to haunt my work, "that's why I asked you over lunch whether you might write about David, I mean, I didn't want you to think my question was gratuitous," and I know immediately what he means & how that is, the way one death can always stand in for another, the way bodies serve as proxies, one loss arousing the memories of all its familiars, and after a moment's pause, at once touched and disoriented by the depth of Bruce's thoughtfulness and care, I tell him how perceptive his insight happens to be as I've been struggling, I say, to grasp some relation, however tenuous—a relation perhaps obvious to my friends but one that's taken me this long to realize—between my own trauma and all the writing I've been doing for years now about sex with fallen soldiers & deceased detainees, a struggle informed by the obvious incommensurability between this and that, on the one hand, and on the other by the fear that the poems might bear the impress of a body more intimate than I've been able to avow, a loss for which my excesses have longed to compensate, and I stumble in my effort to explain, ambivalent and unsure, if not scared of suggesting a link because that would make it real, at which point Bruce completes an idea I can't complete myself. "Yeah, all yr dead ones," he says *un tombeau vide en extase courbeé* as if I were Andromache still bent over her empty grave.

CORRESPONDENCES

Dear Abu Wa'el Dhiab ~

Dav asked if I've written to you directly and it makes me
Afraid I've forgotten something crucial like addressing
This to the place of impossible reception the common

Place being police force & state terror I thought I had
Thought of everything so the question shudders thru
My bowels *fears of fraudulence* like when Tedd asked if

I'd ever shared my porn w/ a soldier but I know yr name
- 's just a placeholder impossible address being fullness
Of relation realized & denied "real contact" just another

False immediacy like direct discourse *idolatry* my poems court
& refuse what passes for communication under these con
- ditions yr body cleaves grammatical norms yielding a poem

- 's forced ~~feelings~~ feedings rectal enemas extralegal rule
So evangelical covered up inside a concrete rape this obscenity
Being both the law & its undoing so y've replaced him

Dear reader the meaning of my writing you

— now cast in doubt.

Dear Muhammed Ahmad ~

There must be a total incompatibility between the idea
Of sending you this letter and the dream of the poem it
- self annuls the difference btwn realist & utopian desire

Being no difference at all I keep dreaming of objects they
Bewilder me *a cop a soldier a detainee* love's radical promise
Blocked at the site of its deviation *a square a cell a sentence*

I just want to go on singing yr body sanctum of my inner
Eye immobile space of autopsy yr remains now scat
- tered deep inside us but the ligature you allegedly used

To sublime into language *relique of yr martyrdom* binds
My cock it's wired to a pulley so you can conduct it
From afar make the thing go up & down tho really

I'm being digitally fucked by a mannequin's cold hand
Casually held by a friend who's more than willing
To oblige a momentary fabrication of need turning

The most transparent acts

       — *opaque.*

Dear Shaker Amer ~

Were my letter to reach you it would destroy conditions
Of the poems' possibility as if a resurrection of yr name
Could stand for something more than mere negation

Of yr personhood illusion of universal address an empty
Formalism like justice itself whose truth the poems otherwise
Belie the way the page becomes a viewfinder it frames

You or yr figure *black odalisque* a gesture of impossible
Repose reclining on a table the exchange of any leather
Cord for one specific elastic band torn from yr army is

- sued panties marks the end of a therapeutic process where
- by one fantasy is successfully replaced by another an end
- less chain transforming my melancholia into a season

- al affective disorder before passing with the snow so I jerk
The thing myself tugging on plastic & string my utopian
Calamari of the camp a terminus where I anchor this

Writing as if yr hand had never been removed

                     — from so commonplace a function.

Dear Hassin Bin Attash ~

As hard as I've tried I fail to narrate our relationship a symptom
Of larger problems like my inner life at least its primary structures
Contracts & debt this unlivable promise our bond maybe this

Is already that mourning the way I've replaced a soldier's prosthetic
With a finely spun catheter forced to enter by way of yr nose
Without lubrication honey or vaseline any organ can be the scene

Of erotic attachment so many unknown pleasures deriving from care
But I'm no longer writing to you perhaps I never was the whole
Situation being this gross charade as my letter assumes qualities

Of a private perversion coeval w/ yr destitution it enacts a world
Phantasms recalling the old cliché of a society woman turned pro
- stitute these truths guaranteed by the falseness of the world

My poems

> *— so many follies in a nature park.*

Dearest Imad Abdullah Hassan ~

You are my inner experience everyday life
Being the space between this letter and its
Impossible reception I mean it's the totality

Of yr abstraction *absence of any image* that keeps
Me coming back for more I'd rather imagine
The waning of desire as it pushes toward

A lost horizon where what I am doing now
Tracing yr figure in a trance will soon be impos
- sible to imagine anything to make my poems

Ridiculous yr body it's like a thing pumped
W/ no image system it precipitates in phrases
"Serial sectioning" "no evidence of trauma"

"Clear of debris & foreign material" "smooth
& unremarkable" when cut you seem to be
Made-up entirely a mass of small seeds

Varying in size from millet to hemp the fact
I continue to conjure such sentences hides
A lie my poems can't combat being nothing

Equal to yr body

— *in labor language or love.*

Dear [——] ~

Look how I keep slipping on the terms of contract
Substituting exchangeable names as if yrs were
Arbitrary anything to get you in my mouth I want

To think there's someone but there's no one there
My longing to recover the pathos of direct address it's
Always imaginary except when repeating the summons

Tribunal truth our shared condition never to be
Shared so I've failed to persevere in this exhaustive
Communication my desire for fusion already real

- ized its repetitions *clear plane of potential visibility*
At once mine and not mine in the end a thin skin
Separates me like an envelope *property fence police tape*

Cordon sanitaire from yr banished excrescence
While opening impossible communions the way
A vague line divides sea & sky sculpture & fog

These contradictory impulses

— reconciled only in dreams.

LATE NITE EMISSIONS

I CONTINUE HAVING wet dreams deep into my adult life. There's no clear reasoning to explain this phenomenon in the medical literature, and I have no concern for what it might mean about my body or my person. However anomalous, my involuntary spasms remain a source of mystery and pleasure, and I marvel at each occurrence. Recently, my nocturnal emissions barely produce even the faintest of secretions *dry orgasm* but this only enhances their intensity. Within the narrative of any one dream, the somatic shudder, coming while asleep, rarely occurs in relation to anything you might call a sexual situation. I could be in line at the Safeway waiting with bread & soap, or at a bank teller's window making a stupid transaction. It's always the pressure to complete a simple task that overwhelms my bulk, which then succumbs to organ functions I can't control as I become publicly incontinent, shitting my linen white pants, like Carrie bleeding in the shower. But it's really nothing like that. It's more like sitting in traffic. Duration is unbearable and there's nothing sexy about it, the experience of time being but a residue of collective labor, material support of detention's sentient figure. Memory is all but flattened and there's nothing to hold on to. Everything's hemorrhaged, organs without bodies lost in an autopsy report. That's how it was last night, for example. I was in the airport for an international flight, a mess on the floor of the departures pavilion, which looks like the main hall of the Grand Palais, vast cavity of a whale. Everything I own is spread around me. Nothing will fit in my fucking bag. The more I stuff, the more stuff accumulates on the airport's ancient mosaic ground. I know I'm going to miss my flight if I don't abandon my things, which I can't seem to do, though I don't recognize my belongings as belonging to me *the lingerie, the bra*. As soon as I begin to panic, I feel a deep and tender stirring in my groin, a slight and constant pressure at the base of my balls *warm as yellow light* as if I have to pee, which in the dream I'm convinced I do, though I can't bring myself to look for a bathroom, knowing that more time lost will result in something consequential I can't discern, the way I can't discern the signs that animate my body. As my organs contract, I feel myself holding back and the effort of maximum retention slows me down even more. But instead of peeing, I come in my pants, having obviously mistaken one sensation for another.

MY WET DREAMS animate a familiar narrative problem: irreconcilable temporalities *time of the organs & time of the schedule, time of the flesh & time of production* the premature resolution of which can only be orgasm. The dissociation of soma and story couldn't be more conspicuous, an abyss between body and world traversed by longing, my tenuous bridge. Last nite, escaping something I still can't name, I felt that stirring in my groin while rushing to meet a bus that I knew would be fatal to miss. In the distance, I make out the destination sign, "UNSPARKABLE," which causes me unspeakable distress. The urgency I feel is dislocated as it concentrates in that word *unsparkable* as if a part of my own body were now lodged in a sign whose meaning hemorrhaged *Baudelaire's filthy swan* but in which I feel the volatile residue of my detainee's "unremarkable genitalia." Sometimes it's like I'm transcribing his autopsy report in my sleep: "The small and large bowels are unremarkable. The urinary bladder is unremarkable and contains clear yellow urine. The inner lining of the esophagus is red-purple to tan and unremarkable." Upon speaking the unsparkable word aloud to myself, it's like a spell's been broken as I'm shocked into banality and the sudden realization that I'd left my jacket in a café down the road, and with it the pocketed key I would need upon my arrival [——]. As if the word *unsparkable* possessed the power to keep me from getting on the bus, I'm turned away and run to retrieve a coat, my limbs slow thru proverbial sludge. The premonition of self-shattering doom becomes the source of amplified gravity, the binding agent of my preservation rapidly eroding, quickening all my organ functions. As I approach the café, there's that stirring in my groin, pulse pressuring prostate, and the sensation of having to pee, something I can't stop to do. Despite the feeling's familiarity *unremarkable* it slows me down even more, enhancing my panic to that pleasantly painful pinch. I'm under strict watch, as the gaze of others penetrates me thru the café windows. Overwhelmed by fear and shame, my inability to arrest the pulse becomes a freely floating pleasure exceeding every constraint, transforming my embarrassment as I lose control on the sidewalk, the intimacy of orgasm entwined with the related horrors of public incontinence and total surveillance.

THE DREAM OPENS on a swank party. Everyone's dressed to the nines—men in black-tie, women in couture—but I'm in t-shirt & shorts. Becoming self-conscious, my embarrassment manifests in the deep feeling of having to shit, and as my embarrassment increases, I rush to find the toilet, which doesn't exist to be found. Unable to hold my bowels, I experience the effort of keeping myself from letting go as a total resistance that becomes my body. Or rather, my body becomes this opaque resistance to forces unwieldy and implacable. "HIS UNREMARKABLE GENITALIA" penetrates the dreamscape, and I see the words rise above my head, like Magritte's pipe, a cartoon caption, or an epithet *fucking faggot* designed to denote my person even as it eludes my grasp. "Unremarkable," I say aloud in my sleep, as if casting a spell to make the insufferable strain in my bowels disappear, and the word cracks open like a piñata. But real relief will only come with humiliation. As the pressure in my groin enflames the sphincter, I contract all my organs to keep from dumping. The feeling blurs with the restraint I might command while having sex were I only better equipped in body & mind to withstand the urge to orgasm prematurely, which is always the case, I mean, I always come too soon, unable to balance the need for temporal release with my desire for dilation, which then gets displaced on my writing. The party is like a glass diorama I can't escape, just as I can't dispel the somatic confusion, which persists despite my awareness of mistaking one organ function for another. There's often that split second when you awaken to the fact that you're dreaming while still under the spell of the dream. Just give in to the pleasure of coming, I say to myself, though I know this will manifest as the pleasure of shitting, a pleasure augmented by public exposure and disgrace. That's when my bowels explode on the party floor and I come in my sleep without touching anything at all. The grammatical conjunction *bowels explode and I come in my sleep* whereby the preceding sentence falls into non sequitur corresponds with a critical moment when the subject of the dream is destroyed *together with "his unremarkable genitalia"* just as the instinct toward self-preservation gives way to its own annihilation, the result of which is not death, but pure affirmation in the breakdown of body & rule.

I KNOW HE'S the one whose report I've been transcribing. We're in a windowless department store that resembles the basement floor of every Ikea, marveling at the vast array of commodities—linen, glass, ceramic, wicker, plastic—when two signs awaken me to the fact that it's really him: the wound below his left nipple in the shape of a bean, which in my dream matches the wound detailed in the report, and the fluorescent waistband of his U.S. Army issued briefs, hot pink, which I know like some kind of pre-cog will become the reported "ligature" with which he'll allegedly hang himself on a redacted date in 2006. While quite secure below his belly, this sash has already left an auratic mark around his neck. We're naked except for our shoes and this one accouterment. Everyone is speaking Arabic, and I experience a strange rush that I can't identify. Unable to avert my gaze from his groin, the word "remarkable" escapes from under my breath as if I were attempting to give a name to a thing for which no adequate name exists *what would it feel like to name the sky "sky" for the first time* but my act of authentic nomination succumbs to its modifier, the way my love falls prey to whatever narrative awaits it. In a quick cut, I find myself sitting alone, still naked, on a faux leather couch in one of the mock-up living rooms on the upper floor. "It's pleather," I hear him say in a whisper that reaches me from the basement, as though he were simply reiterating a domestic agreement to keep bad materials out of our home. I'm reading Georges Perec's book of dreams, *Boutique*

Obscure, wherein I find my own dream marvelously predicted, when I feel that stirring in my groin *sympathetic magic* like I have to pee, but with scores of shoppers suddenly milling about, I'm unable to move to relieve myself. I can't decide whether I remain seated because I'm glued to the spot against my will, or because I know that my job as mannequin is linked to the fate of my Pakistani husband—detained indefinitely, and perhaps already dead—whose future hangs on my ability to occupy the role of stationary model. It doesn't take long for me to realize that I don't have to pee, and am in fact about to come in full view of every passerby on a busy shopping day. The intensity of pressure is matched only by my longing for him to make it up from house wares in time to watch me explode. I look down and see that I don't even have a hard-on—am not even touching myself—but I orgasm nonetheless *no friction* producing a feeling at once unbearable and exquisite.

[————] and I are naked and on display in a little storefront, like the one at ATA on Valencia Street, where the Right Window collective mounts its shows. We're publicly bruising one another with blunt instruments: toy hammers, wood blocks, baby dumbbells. I'm amused by the playfulness of our choreographed sparring and figure we must be staging some kind of performance. Everyone is watching *total surveillance* as the bruises begin to appear on our skins. Proprioceptive disorientation *looking at his limbs and feeling my own* makes it difficult for me to determine whose bruise is whose, as if his organs were inside me, the way his gestures, too, inhabit my flesh, making the phrase "my own" a stupidity, and this is an ecstasy as every body in history might as well be touching mine. Above our heads, images of each contusion appear, vague splotches of purple light whose contours blur to white. Inside bruise-light there hovers, superimposed, a phrase of anatomical language, like the inscription-bearing blobs and thick voluminous masses in Magritte's *Personnage marchant vers l'horizon*, each word floating unhinged from the fleshy thing where it's inscribed. "Moderately firm subcutaneous fat layer" hovers above a patch of red-brown light, a projection of my bruised arm after he swings at me gleefully with a pot. "Bilaterally descended unremarkable testes" appears inside a shape whose model is my swollen ass. One by one our bruises appear, nothing more than shape & color, as things fail to resemble. "Renal capsules smooth and thin." "Nasal skeleton palpably intact." "Body temperature cold due to refrigeration." "Asphyxia due to ligature strangulation." In the dream, I read this language as corporate branding, our bodies subjugated to slogans of production, as if this were the message we'd intended our art to communicate, which I pretend I've understood all along. This is how the dream dreams its frame, as the body finds its semantic support in the dark recesses of organ and sinew, linguistic space of a corpse *forced individuation* whose interior is inseparable from my own. A final screen of clinical abstraction *universal language* fails each particular case whose liquidated person I've resurrected as my lover. In the middle of our performance, I get that odd sensation in my groin *familiar enough to console, strange enough to startle* and I panic, not wanting to fall into orgasm, which would end the ecstasy by throwing me out of my dream. Instead, I convince myself I have to pee. I shudder because everyone is watching and I don't want to interrupt the show to take a leak. As the feeling grows in intensity, I can barely stand, let alone continue to swing the bat I'm using to parry his loving blows. I'm unable even to turn my back to the street *conceal that erection* given my commitment to the choreography we'd rehearsed. That's when I feel myself starting to come, paralyzed with pleasure and mourning.

I AM PREGNANT with his child. I know this, and though my detainee isn't even in the dream, his body haunts every detail of it, and my baby is his. The saturation of this scene with his absence is extreme. He's in every mote of dust and I'm engulfed by it as each relation teeters unmoored, unanchored to a stable name. Though absent, he's omnipresent. Identities dissociate, as if he were me, plus everything else. Even the gurney where I'm stationed for prenatal care has absorbed his identity, which is no identity at all, a specter of a name shared by everyone, his autopsy having become the universal shape of things. Even the body I take to be my own is also his, making the "I" a grammatical fallacy, and to say "my body" would be as strange as saying "my land," "my air," "my water." So we enter a small closet, an x-ray chamber or ultrasound cabinet. You can hear the thing speak from inside the belly: How is this going to happen?, it says. The fetus's use of the future tense is curious given the impossibility of what's happening in the present, which is no present at all, but a time-sponge that becomes the dream. Upon exiting the cabinet, the fetus manifests outside, though the body remains pregnant. The alien form is sexless, wrapped tight in a richly textured swaddling cloth whereby it remains secure. How will you conceive?, it asks and again the tense seems confused, making it impossible to utter a word, as if grammar had created a fold in time where language hardens. The ligature, I answer to myself, as though the word alone possessed generative power. Then, like an echo of my inner voice, "the ligature" resounds from nowhere, an acoustic image with no referent in the dream, though supplementing it with this fundamental part, binding the whole together. But rather than naming something, "the ligature" plots a body displaced and penetrates the world. How will you conceive?, the fetal lump asks again, which my dream writing edits retrospectively and replaces with "How have you conceived it?" concealing the temporal error. There's only an echo, this erosion of sound, key to my conception, "the ligature," a sonic cover or a cord connected to my lumpen drape, dangling as umbilicus, wrapped around my cock. Upon waking, I feel for the band, and in its absence I experience the distance separating me from my detainee as the distance separating me from myself, a measure strangely commensurate with the length of this sentence.

WALKING ALONG THE Canal Saint-Martin, I begin to weep while listening to Yo La Tengo's "Alyda." It's hard to account for the abundance of feeling aroused by the perfection of back-up harmony and chord structure, but the song stirs a space between organs *where mourning lives* leaving my pleasure centers broken. This occurs just after having located, over my morning coffee, the Joint Task Force's updated Standard Operating Procedure regarding the enteral feeding of Gitmo detainees. I'd suspected that the autopsied suicide whose report I've been transcribing had resorted to the ligature only after having had his voluntary cessation of self-nourishment *hunger strike* torturously interrupted with forced feeding, but my tears have nothing to do with this. After reading the document, I took to the canal for a walk and, ever-suspicious of my own work, I was scrutinizing the use to which I've pressed the autopsy report, as well as my relation to the body that its language denotes. That's when "Alyda" throws my gut into zones of unharnessed affect, stimulating this rush of mottled memory in excess of any referent. My first love, James, died while I was in this city, half a world away from him, back in 1995, a death for which I've yet to forgive myself, as if I could have prevented catastrophe had I only been there by his side, and this loss continues to inhabit my writing. So it's been about mourning all along, I say to myself. "I feel so ashamed of still living when J. is dead, and it causes me great suffering which rises to my surface," writes Genet in *Funeral*

Rites, a novel I've made my own. "You're getting off among candles," I continue from memory, and wonder whether it's possible to write about love and loss in this city, itself a fiction of apperception, bloated with sentiment secreted from books and films. Aroused by a song, the faucet opens and I can't manage the pressure. If you're going to lose it, don't be mawkish, I tell myself, as if I were about to throw myself to the ground, my pain so great as it seeks escape in the form of fiery gestures, like Genet's narrator, or Hecuba still mourning on the burning ramparts of Troy, neck craned back, face hidden in the crook of her arm. For a moment, all these feelings mingle as if the associations that unleashed them were immediate and true and not the effect of a contingent force, like "Alyda," under the spell of whose alchemic fusion every one of my emotions empties its content into a common grave where it's impossible to recover anything specific from the feelings aroused by a pop song so fantastically wedding me to James's skin, as if I could still taste it. The pain of thinking about him now as I write brings tears to my eyes, whereas my suffering had borne exquisite pleasure under "Alyda"'s bridge. This is both true and false. True because the song mysteriously lends expression to real separation, our riven bodies, casualty of history, which bears down unevenly on my objects. False because the distance between the things we live among has been transformed under the spell of a song, smoothed into unitary space, the sensation being one of resurrected union, which my body swallows, recalling blissful identity, my romance of nature and myth. Dreaming the same, this is when I sense that pressure at the base of my balls and feel myself about to come, the radical disjunction of body function and objective stimulus making this an allegory of sexuality in its purest form, moving in a space of contradiction and fantasy, disengaged from any proper aim. The intensity of my little frenzy is inseparable from some repression *lubricant for accumulation* as my organs become enflamed with his *whose?* spectacular absence. The orgasm lasts a ridiculously long time *I can't stop coming* though I release very little fluid.

SOUND & SENSE escape me, so the exchange must be telepathic as my dream brings soft focus to his unremarkable genitalia. My detainee asks the guard, who could only be myself (there being no other human figure present) to close his "bean hole cover." As this language penetrates my unconscious, curious phrases & riddles must be either cracked or literalized. Loner lid. Feed slot. Floor mat. Organ aid. Cell drape. Peep hole. Box top. Can seat. A floating dish of dried legumes—desiccating kidney beans—becomes my visual association in calligraphic union with the scene, the way his quiet supplication arouses my longing. Strange geometric patterns hover between us, the sensation of touch made visible, a hole turned inside out. All obscure things come to an end when his uselessness arrives at total feeling. Our communication seems to hang on the significance of what can't be deciphered, so I cradle him, pressed, at the limit of what my poem won't permit, giving myself to orders whose source subjects me to a phrase. Words withdraw along the horizon of my fantasy [——] where contraries rush and contradictions collapse, the way the security of his protective flap has its corresponding gesture in a bland disrobing. Discovery calls for tender measures. This is how a "bean hole cover" becomes my dream, a neon sign whose electric current induces pictures, infusing the sensorium with its soporific glow. Meaning eludes my grasp, a prophylactic against every common place, clear indication that he's ready to sleep. What would it mean to recover this phrase for common sense, restore each organ vanished in its closure. I'm struggling to ask this—anything to voice, a smothered yelp, a whimper, or something concerning his bowels—when I get that familiar tingle in my groin and reach for the latrine, dragging myself just close enough to smell the crap he left an hour ago. Casting my eyes inside the bowl, my mouth becomes the toilet's drain, my tongue lifting up from metal expanse as if to rim his hole, which would be my own, I suppose, were I able to sit, my body simultaneously splayed and whole, like his. This must account for my vocal block and the awkward feeling that I'm going to shit inside my maw, still wanting that. But instead, I come in my sleep, benignly without waking. Inside his bean hole cover, the world's unrecognizable, but the meaning of my dream remains contained by the camp's circumference. His body might disrupt a more aggressive sadism, I think, but my kisses will never taste the sweetness of so detained a tongue, as the vacuum of my most pacific gesture equals the space of his cell. Still longing for his hair, having come full circle, my comrade I wrapped in his blanket, enveloped well his form, etc., etc…

ABUNDANCE WASHED

THERE ARE SO many things I've failed to tell you, things I'm still dying to share without quite knowing how. Even all my wet dreams speak of what I can't perceive around which something hardens into sense, the way my cock once hardened in a soldier's wound, another common place *totally banal* like the body of my detainee, or the pen that keeps him still. I know I've told you too much about all this already and it's coming back to haunt, as if the chokepoint thru which the system moves were a hole in my bowels still being plugged by a private's hot device, limit of what this structure can imagine about itself. But that was another time and place, whereas now, I have to poach a feeding tube or the elastic band of his stupid briefs, anything to pinch the place of passage and arouse a shameless pleasure. This cord around my balls *like my poem* belies a mannered style. It's only a question of relation between value and flesh, another false immediacy like the "thing itself," which can only be grasped as a circulation process. But I can't sing the pleasures of merely circulating because those pleasures would require an explanation of substitution, the way one proper name yields to another, my unavowable economy. These past few days I haven't stopped thinking about him, a mourning so vulnerable to the substitution of names. I can tell you this is all related to the movement between my bed and U.S. black sites, from the Salt Pit in Afghanistan to Bound Steel in Kosovo, then on to Guantanamo Bay, but I still can't tell you how. Does his cell reek of the old carbolic soap and rectal mucus, or is that me, the way my inner sanctum could be anyone's when it burns. Access barred, I fantasize relation where relation's been disfigured, together with the body's vital processes, a strangeness haunted by our intimacy, no image to secure it. "Real love's impersonal," equal in extremity to what imprisons and tortures. Once again, I've eroticized the obstacle to communization, dreaming of an easy liquidation. During the time of writing this, I've been receiving signs from that once rumored place, soft phonemes muffled deep in sleep, tics now grafted to my flesh, some language in the air whose implication exceeds my reach, strange music lacking audible measure but against whose staff I press my song. His body's severed ties surpass sensation, like the financial sublime, a source of clarity whose shadow is misery, my occulted union a thing of waste ensuring ground rent, nomos of the earth, this theater of displacement, perjured as the stars. And when the circuit is complete, his body ceases to be a body and becomes our mode of existence. Despite this appearance of exceptional vacancy, his inner life shares something of quality *plenitude* with the interior of my car, the site of his abandonment, coextensive with everything I own, the way immiseration concentrates deep inside these artichokes. My briefs get wet just thinking about his hair, the radicality of his unremarkable genitalia, or my poems themselves, whatever blocks the road to becoming money. The feeling's all tingly at first, then I lose control of my bowels, the tender tissue from throat to rectum stretching like Saran along a windy plain awaiting any sensation whatever as I harden with his body's withdrawn parts, or at least my sentence does, as if his mucus were really mine, longing for a common good. Structured by force, the public face of unknown pleasures, what do these fantasies in fact portend, I ask myself daily on the bus from downtown to the city's satellite health center as I map my digestion onto mass transit routes where need looks like nature, the way light shoots thru his ureters as a pure yellow urine settles into pixilated sight, a detention cell and its autopsied corpse, a vaporous fringe, like bodies in a square, organized stress, commodious resource, utopian bait converging with its own erasure. But my body's harnessed to more hygienic interiors *food court at Target, baggage claim at Laguardia* which facilitate the logic of police, the way rendition and detention follow like points in a chain, cause and effect removed from their conditions, pegs to bolt a process, the way any part—say a bulb or screw made somewhere in China—is flown to service ballistics in Idaho. My own airs mime a swollen cant, the inner sleeve of some report, while his remains externalize the commons. And if it's true that the commons is not a thing but a relation, then I need to represent my attachment to his eclipsed form as something more than conservation of a detained object. He's my inner essence, the truth my body apes when every corpse in history is mine. And so, in a kind of radical mimicry *sympathetic magic* I spread my cheeks and await the tube whose insertion prefigures the future of authenticity where any hint of originality becomes criterion for kitsch. As the intensity of pleasure grows, I conjure pictures to block the way to climax. It's gotten to the point where I can barely make myself come, being the disruption of thought, a delirium in which I lose my safe word, a vague communication, realized labor of consumption. What community will emerge in so negative a place without being sentenced in advance? It's a little like asking what form a friendship must assume to lubricate revolt and not its consolation. These questions enhance the hardship of orgasm, a steady anaesthetization, strange structure of my feeling, enchanting disenchantment with the hope that I might arouse you too if only by rubbing myself against the poem's conceptual purity, like a horny dog or cat. Patrolling the limits of popular speech, my sentence, lame residue of rhetorical force, seeks a gesture to exceed the force that produced it. All this happened to me yesterday, the excitement I felt fondling his cock whose erection confirms my inclusion in the world's plenty. Even his body appears as a dynamic reaction to surface events only visible on other surfaces distant from it. No doubt, my theory of history sounds like an app for yr phone, the way his figure disappears in the space between two screens, like Smithson's removal of the picture plane in his *Enantiomorphic Chambers*, a structure that actually "sees nothing," he writes, which reminds me of Emmanuel Riva in *Hiroshima mon amour* and I wonder if I could ever make a poem attuned to do the same. In other words, something gets lost in the space between my fantasy of fucking and the future of corn, this being inseparable from the future of finance, though I can't tell you exactly how. I admit, I've been struggling to get the world of banking into my poem *there, I guess I did it* but this isn't quite the same as getting a detainee inside, which is much more difficult, I mean, the world of banking is in the writing whether I want it to be or not and to name it as such is less a debunking than a mere restating of the obvious. Like the homosexual necrophilia often noted in the mallard duck, this demonstration of feeling gets me no closer to the fugitive beauty I'm after. Fate being a future's market, maybe this is what I've been meaning to tell you all along, the way my face breaks out when I imagine his body, which is no body when I'm not imagining it, and whose distance collapses, a star inside my heart going nova, before fading to black. The odor of his anal mucus is sublime but the sentence that transfigures it can't escape the decorative, its language being nothing more than the actuality of that estrangement, my desire cast in bronze. But when his body fails to be distinguished from its material support I guess it's fair to say he's been sufficiently fucked. So what's the point of having the right idea when "right" itself has become obscene. I mean, it's impossible to recognize myself except in the figure policing his cell. Pasolini's right, sex is just an allegory for bodies at the hands of power, but I want to turn love into a miracle play. For example, lying two inches above a red-hot flame, his limbs, now frightfully dislocated, slowly melt as his trunk is lowered into a brazier, allowing me time to carve away several chunks of flesh selected from diverse areas. I'm then obliged to burn the interior of his rectum, which I've fucked without pomade before discharging and falling half-conscious into an armchair. This is the moment where my lucid mind inhabits his skin, producing phantoms degraded into matter like a concrete slab, which I've tried to render real. All of my writing problems are confirmed by the office of mortuary affairs whose organic language thrives in dark places, clear of debris and foreign material, focal lesions, smooth mucosa, velvety bowels, the common good lodged in a gulf between aura and meat from which I've liberally borrowed, necessary for replacement at any moment in the circuit of consumption. But in order for this fantasy to succeed, subject and object positions must be reversible contradicting my own recombinant opportunities, swappables bundled by the voice, so many feelings hovering just beyond my grasp and failing to consolidate as thought, a collapse of value in things unreal. So when nite falls on autopsy whose clarity renders his organs stately, my work falls under the sign of dumb experiment as the use of every word cleaves its common place behind a sanitary cord where my poem hardens like a twig, mere artifact of nature, a branch of seaweed deformed by the sun the way sand turns to glass and glass to rock, rock to bone and bone to nail,

nail to dust and dust to hair, a lock whose strands I've woven thru these pages, his body having passed thru an Ovidian dream, prelude to a place our present had all but sabotaged, then sabotaged.

NOCTURNAL RESIDUA

READING THESE POEMS in public makes me feel sick.

The venue is Salt & Cedar, a letterpress print shop where Matvei's doing a residency in Detroit's Eastern Market. I'm happy to be on the bill with Johannes Göransson & Christian Hawkey, and they both read well, but the conversation following our readings is strained, barely concealing our discomfort. I hate this part. There's talk of Kathryn Bigelow's film, the obvious link between militarized torture & S/M in the social imaginary, which *Zero Dark Thirty* totally exploits, I guess, by reproducing it as spectacle, or B-movie kitsch, Johannes says, which makes me think of Genet's campiness, at whose limit the extravagance of gesture gives way to purity of purpose, something I want to channel, the excess of that affect, give it body, arouse relation at the common place *the camp* where relation is prohibited, negate an alienation whose effects I'm feeling even now as I write, reaching for something beyond the current containment, something banished or withdrawn but from which the system nevertheless draws its energy, something that can't be admitted except allegorically, say, in the figure of a soldier's wound or my detainee's unremarkable genitalia, these things without reference, his body on a table, a radical thing betrayed on contact with my sentence, where syntax renders everything the same.

I hate this part. A sucker for the shame my poems outrun, though still prone to feeling sick with it, public events like this work as purest bait, and my Gitmo poems only amplify the feeling, a fear of offense turning inward, then back to ectoplasm seeking orifice & release.

I want to believe the writing needs to be written, not that it simply can be, though I'm allergic to the effects this need creates and break out in a rash, acne or hives, an autoimmune response where my body rejects a product it fails to recognize as its own. So this is my wasting syndrome, I think, as the language of autopsy amplifies the signs my Propranolol is prescribed to mask: the swollen tongue & quickened pulse, the noisome sweat & paralyzing hesitation. What troubles me now as I write is the suspicion that my trouble has nothing whatever to do with my detainee's unremarkable genitalia, my symptoms having detached themselves from his body altogether as my body performs this hysteria, rectum released as he melts in nitrous film flesh (that's Burroughs) and I feel myself withdraw to a world of private sensations *opposite of love* betraying my poems' effort to perceive the thing we share.

But in what sense are my sensations private? That's Wittgenstein, whose question is crucial to me now as I become aware of my own beetle & box routine, you know, the one where everyone has a box and in it there's something we've all agreed to call "beetle" without knowing what's in anyone else's box *hoax of all true knowledge* a private affair belied by a word. There can be no private language, so the argument goes. What happens, though, when the box is a cell we all share and in it there's a body we'll never see but whose intense existence demands that it be felt without being named (that's Stein). So my earnestness becomes embarrassment as I invest a common place with authentic feeling, his unremarkable genitalia, laying myself bare for similar accusations of kitsch *extortion of sentiment* as my own genitals sense their banality. And in that humiliation, narration only falters, the way my rehearsal of any wet dream might, but at least the latter ends in orgasm.

After a cigarette with Matvei, pleasant to a point given the sweetness of his company, I feel sick and await the familiar pressure in my groin as if I were about to shit or come and I brace myself but nothing happens, because this is not a dream, it's a poem.

Finding myself beside my friend Melissa, I ask her what she thought of the reading because I can't stop obsessing, and she says, "I can only imagine how much fun it must be to be yr penis," which only intensifies my embarrassment as if this were about my so-called sex life at all, as if my penis had any thing to do with it, as if, like Genet's narrator, "I can oppose the stiffness of his corpse with the stiffness of my prick," confusing *my* prick with its fictitious proxy. But then again, maybe I *do* want it both ways, the exaggerated *idea* of my cock, dumb instrument whose rhetoric of sensation mediates a perception of relation with otherwise unrelatable things, recalling the way another poet I know once wrote a whole book about "his" dick lifting a lot of stupid shit in his apartment, bad joke of masculine prerogative, which is sadly also mine.

In my dream later that nite, Matvei finds a spider built like a set of drink coasters, which unfolds from a well-designed holster, like something you'd find in a high-end 70s home furnishings rag, before the thing combusts in yellow fusion, mustard pollen settling on shag beneath the vitrine where we're doing our taxonomy lesson. But this is not a dream, it's a poem. There's no stirring at the base of my balls, no pressure in the rectum, no tingle at the perineum, and I wake on the verge of panic, mortified not by the language of gastric mucosa, the red-brown cortical surfaces of the urinary bladder and the pancreas with its pink-tan lobulated appearance, nor the extraordinarily rendered bodies thereby denoted. Rather, I feel sick from having read my poems at Salt & Cedar about being fucked by my enemy combatant, an experiment in fidelity to the object status of things. *Hoc est corpus.* But even my shame becomes allegorical, a floating feeling detached from the poems' referent, his unremarkable genitalia, negated in being positively tagged and to which I cling publicly in bad faith.

So I begin to masturbate, knowing that short of pills orgasm alone might release the endorphins and allow me to sleep, or rather I begin writing my Nocturnal Residua in an effort to overcome that bad faith. This is how the body of a detainee, around whose figure I've forged a fantasy so that I might feel the unrelatable limit of my world, gives way to the body of one "Christian Hawkey," whose proper name particularizes my fantasy, lending it a searchable imprimatur, promise of ownership & trade. His body performs the manly tricks I fall for every time *ideal of a soldier* whose codified norm presumes *falsifies* a universal content, dominant charge my poems mean to defy. But I really do need to get-off and his masculine frame works like a charm, enflames my cock as my desire betrays its conservative core *self-preservation* materializing shame in a shot of cum *or the sentence that presents it* abject limit of my writing's usefulness. His meaty forearm alone is enough to keep my focus, the way it grazes my thigh as I bury my head in his hairy crotch and approach the limit of my poems, giving the lie to my longing which I publicize for you here in an effort to resist it being privatized. "Abu Ahmad Al Hanashi" can't do what "Christian Hawkey" can. And yet, the bodies denoted by these ciphers interpenetrate in some fundamental way *the names as if identical, mediated by the same whole (this too being false)* each animating the other's defining edge as I organize my love behind a detainee's idealized anonymity.

    This is not a wet dream, it's a poem, and I want to believe it needs to be written, not simply that it can be. But the degree to which my writing sublimes in private yearning is the degree to which it yields to civic embarrassment. That my fantasy of "Christian Hawkey" inspires more humiliation than the one in which I'm fucked by a detainee confuses me even more than reading these poems in public. Or is it just the way his name appears to laminate my lust to an identifiable body only properly desired when tagged advertising its particularity *false virtue of a name* negating the utopia of my detainee's unremarkable genitalia.

        Now render this fantasy as a common place whose structure of feeling we share:

"The dead remains too nothing. / What will we do till nightfall?"
(That's Auden.) So when masturbation fails, I work
Transcribing autopsy reports because I want to
Merge with you and in merging become not one
The way the myth reassures but limitless as I fulfill
The promise of my individual person in this infinity
Of military hardware & online shopping whose auto
- nomous value informs my inner life, illuminates
The body viewed thru a cell window where he lay
Not breathing. Reported to be in that fetal position
Covered with a blanket, head slightly tilted, hands
& feet exposed when the guards enter to secure my
Decedent's swollen tongue, I notice the defining

Thing, a ligature consisting of an elastic band tightly
Wrapped at least twice around his neck, twisted
On the left, having to be cut from the same. At approx
- imately 2200 hours he asks for a nurse, requests a sleep
- ing pill and is last known alive 10-15 minutes later
When he calls for the guard to close his "bean hole
Cover," a sign meaning he's ready to sleep. A few
Minutes later he's discovered unmoved & unresp
- onsive. That's when I enter to sponge his brow
Before wrapping the ligature around my cock secur
- ing the thing at the base of my balls where the press
- ure keeps me hard as I caress his head on my thigh
Close my eyes and sing.

                        Because unlike "a clerk
Cataloging the results of a premise" (that's Sol LeWitt)
I admit libidinal impulses otherwise subtracted from
The record, like extraneous sensations, the real smell
Of rectal mucus, my organs touching the social limit
His body, "blunt indefatigable fact" (that's Sylvia Plath)
If only to pit report against its administration
Stifle the sound of autopsy's universal tongue
By including swollen things outside the image or be-
- yond the imaginable like someone's shiver in de Sade

Whose perversion is nothing but an empty place
In the order of property an unspeakable name
That is no name and will never be proper and whose
Dirtiness makes it common or whose banality
Makes it sleazy like Justine's shudder banned the way
A fake name exceeds obligation to service virtue
- 's four detained boys in succession as they tie me
With strings attached to every part and pull at will
And I sway & lose balance on the edge of losing my
Self the way they introduce stones & pipes to each
Hole whose emptiness opens on unthinkable pleasure
The way exuberance destroys the one who narrates
It there being no common subject as all human me
- asure dissolves, withdrawn inside his cell.

How to rate reality against such make-believe? Can a fantasy of demilitarized enchantment disenchant a militarized fantasy whose opacities circulate as self-evident goods, the effluvia of my productive hours made concrete in his corpse? So I close my eyes and see "Christian Hawkey," who has taken the place of my detainee, and I get on with my ritual, which I needn't rehearse for you further. "That's Emily Dickinson," he interjects repeatedly during his reading in a voice burnished with sampled debris recursively looped & scored for stylized effect, offering my sentence what it needs to get hard. I have my own tricks, which I long here to exhaust or ruin for future use. And so I take his manly frame as my object and approach the limit of my book in his remarkable genitalia. I guess I'm dreaming on the page now, a space that bears no legible resemblance to the common place I write about, but whose open structure is its inverse and complement. It's this substitution that fascinates & troubles, as if I were testing a thesis that love depends not on precision the way my verse supposedly ought to depend, and our bombing believes it does, but rather on something more capacious and unsettling. I'm just trying to adapt in advance to a change in conditions that has yet to arrive, disentangling my interior from the objective conditions that create and deform it. What does it mean to love inside a system that has made love monstrous, to communize this eros. There on my knees, head buried between whose imagined legs, this sentence can't locate our tongues. I rim, I am rimmed: reversible grammar of my commune, whose place the name "Christian Hawkey" usurps as our shared vulgarity disappears in this noiseless white void, a cubicle against whose drywall I hurl exhausted tropes, these tricks that can't save us.

    I hate this part, the way a name displaces the poem's content by becoming it. Aroused inside this excess, I seek comfort in devotional kink. I want to believe the writing needs to be written not that it simply can be, which is what I tell Joseph over lunch at that little Thai joint off of Washington Square. The difference between "my detainee" and "Christian Hawkey" hangs on the difference between purpose and abjection, I say, and it's in abjection *private shame* that my work can only fail, giving into a solitude meaningful to no one but myself. I'm commenting on Joseph's recent book, *The New York School*, with its arousal of so many proper names, a recycling trend, naming names, a symptom of irreconcilable tendency & tenderness, I say, a promise of love feeding on itself when the world grows small and the way we commune struggles to make a viable politics without discharging on the page *I love you Christian Hawkey for you could be anyone* this being the meanness of spirit and not mean-spirited. Still, it happens without any sense of purpose, Joseph says, as if the poems just appear on their own, hanging on these points of intensity, I think, every name a bit of drag, or a privacy setting I need to turn off. Yeah, it's sort of like dreaming, I add, recalling my late nite emissions, and the poems feel it as they begin to sense their own conditions, in which case my language

— *is not a private one at all.*

TO BURN WITH LOVE

(A Suite)

•

If the ban is a form of devotion
What might it mean to burn my so
- vereign nothing you are arrives

At any solid fact to fuel yr body
Even this being a thing created
By suspension of rule my inner

Life being the incorporation
Of yr remains this waste
My filthy residue the poem

Being matter

— lacking yr substance.

•

As if the exceptional site of violence could be
- come the place of sovereign love where to love
You can only mean to waste that love to love

You recklessly staging yr abandonment
In advance

        — *of every utterance.*

•

But sovereignty's so overrated
When it's all been enclosed
Security

— 's what's killing us.

•

The point of communism being to develop
These contradictions when all that is common
Melts into the thinnest ice this cap or crust

Yr despoiled skin a hoary sublimation of ground
Resource ensures a way of life that has no
Life outside yr cage to break the secret bond

Guarantor of smooth functioning like shame
It exacerbates its own conditions so to love
You shamelessly must be

— *the way of this development.*

•

To call the stuff between yr skin & bone bare
Life repeats the violence at the level of concept

Instead of making this abstract limit
Carnal even soma once meant

        — *corpse.*

•

The way Lewis put it over pancakes
& coffee w/ Anna that morning in Madison
My obscene attachment only buries its part

- cular referent inside a fantasy and if
That fantasy is to be faithful to the radical
By which I mean its root in the social

Imaginary it can only be a general thing like
Property my repetitions skip like a court
Record they merely enhance his fundament

- al absence a blank or break becoming
Structure the way my syntax transforms
Its own particularity

— here inside a common sense.

•

You are my common name
But it could be anyone's
And if yr body is not

Even yrs to love you meaning
- fully can only mean
To risk what I am

The loving solution being this

— dissolution of the lover.

CODA
for Sianne

There's nothing more politically transcendent
Said porn director & founder of Treasure
Island Studio than a cheap whore. It was

In an interview I found myself reading one
Afternoon in Dolores Park while thinking
About how to end this book which seems not

To want to end and he goes on by saying
That the body of the true whore is the flint
That makes the spark of revolution

Possible. Is this the spark I have in mind
When considering what it might mean to burn
With love for my detainee and I'm reminded

Of Baudelaire who in The Salon of 1859 writes
(And I can only paraphrase) it's not without
Some reason that I use the word fantasy

Which is all the more dangerous he says when
Unconstrained like the love inspired by a pro
- stitute as it falls into idiocy or degradation.

Fantasy throws light upon the obscurity
That obtains in things he goes on and if it does
- n't then the fantasy is horribly useless

Une inutilité horrible he calls it as if the promise
Of fantasy were strangely one to demystify
A mystified world wherein obscurity reigns or

To disenchant the enchanted while enchanting
That disenchantment in song. So if my song
Appears defiled perhaps it's only failed to shine

A light on its object to penetrate the appearance
Of things whose seeming transparency trans
- figures a useless horror whose own obscure

Abstraction is the use

       — to which it has been put.

POSTSCRIPT:
ON DEVOTIONAL KINK

Better to assume the risk of "evil" than subscribe to this abstract good which drags so many abstract horrors in its wake.

Simone de Beauvoir, "Must We Burn Sade?"

As an experiment in early 2013, I began transcribing the 2009 autopsy report of a Yemini man who had been held in U.S. custody since December 2001, and detained at Guantanamo Bay. Among other things, I wanted to return transcription to its roots in somatic practice, to bring my body into contact with the linguistic remains of extraordinary rendition and state-sponsored death, like a scribe reproducing Torah or a monk laboring over illuminated books unable to restrain himself from spilling into the text. How would my writing *prosthetic of nerve & bone* metabolize such language in an effort to perceive my body's relation to a detainee's occulted corpse? And how might that effort allow me to feel the militarization that has captured our social relations?

The report entered the public sphere, together with a cache of others, by way of the ACLU's recourse to the Freedom of Information Act, and is among the documents that I accessed while working on a book called *Music for Porn* for which I'd been seeking evidentiary language to denote the bodies of fallen U.S. soldiers in Afghanistan and Iraq. At that time, I decided *not* to use any of the language from these Gitmo reports in my soldier porn, afraid that I'd be betraying a fundamental difference, equating the non-equatable, reducing irreducible bodies to the common denominator of stately reportage *bodies made fungible by search engine* despite the fact that any meaningful fidelity to this constraint would be impossible given the functional nomenclature of such reports, the way a curious expression quickly belies a cliché *assembled phrase convenient for the setter of moveable type* linguistic version of the readymade, a common place. For example, a detainee's "unremarkable genitalia," semantic residue of the waste his body has become *autonomous product of security* might mark the gulf between clinical expression and radical sensation, occulted specificity and familiar designation, rupture of word and world.

But how incommensurable are these bodies, really? How mutually exclusive the wounds?

In his *Rhetoric,* Aristotle distinguishes between the "special places" [*topoi idioi*] and "common places" [*topoi koinoi*] of discourse. For Aristotle, distorted utterances *looking sadly at my cock, his balls snipped off with a pair of scissors* constitute the "special places," poetic figures, turns of phrase, singular remarks and idiolectic confections appropriate in some spheres of social intercourse but inappropriate in others. Opposed to "common places," which Aristotle refers to as linguistic expressions that lend themselves to any situation and upon which so-called common sense depends, such perverted locutions by contrast mark scenes of pleasure and suffering whose expression arguably maps the limit of an otherwise shared language. These particular phrases *deaf to common sense* may sound filthy, but for Aristotle they are proper and anything but common.*

While such forms of speech may be necessary for representing our imagined relations to real conditions *themselves so grotesque* or to demystify the ordinary, Aristotle's distinction begs the question as to whether his "unremarkable genitalia" would be among the *topoi koinoi* or the *topoi idioi*. Does such a phrase support a generally valid logic or does it cleave to something "proper"? Like the camp itself: is it common or exceptional?

The appearance of the proper *belonging to one* conceals the communal *shared by all* and this may be the lie of poetry, something ordinary veiled as exceptional. How, then, to dispel that appearance, remove the shroud of property that blithely turns *perversely transfigures* the

---

* I rely here on Paolo Virno's discussion in "Common Places and 'General Intellect'": http://eipcp.net/transversal/0605/virno/en

common place into a special place of meaning? How to make his unremarkable genitalia as ordinary as Homer's rosy-fingered dawn *shorn of its saffron cloak* to return his extraordinarily rendered body *vivisected* to the public square, to conjure communion at the site of its negation, to realize this place *rumored to have been Sodom* as the common place of lost good, anything to prove the proper false.

But as Caleb points out to me, it's already an ideological "common place" to think of Guantanamo as a "special place." "And anyway, isn't *security* not *sovereignty* the common place of the second decade of the war on terror?," he asks. Yeah, I think, like the way local police have been so grotesquely militarized with billions in weapons and vehicles previously used in Afghanistan and Iraq, as that sovereign zone of exception—the camp—becomes coextensive with everywhere *spectacularly realized in Ferguson* canceling the common place in becoming it. By a related logic, my transgressive phrases realize their own banality in their effort to turn the common place into a utopia of total insecurity *rupture of enclosures* to realize a desire for communion *renunciation of immunity* this risk of total relation.

This reminds me of something Brian said when it was snowing and we were on the road to the Museum of Contemporary Art Detroit where Lee was to give his talk on the Mike Kelley Mobile Homestead, a facsimile of Kelley's childhood home in suburban Detroit commissioned and installed in the museum's Midtown yard, a work Lee reads as a return of the repressed, safe refuge for the uncanny specter of white flight. The snow was pretty bad that morning and Lee was trying hard to focus on driving leaving me to talk with Brian who asks, So what if your Gitmo detainee were the body of a black man imprisoned just down the road at Macomb? Or more to the point, I say, what if his body had been shot in the street and left to bake and whose image saturated the public square. As if my own subjectivity were not already an effect of *that* love, an idea I recall from Baldwin, for whom we—black and white—must *like the lovers we already are* end the racial nightmare that is America, a promise of communion, to negate the conditions of radical negation and in doing so abolish the need for my song and its singer. "I use the word 'love' here not merely in the personal sense," he writes in *The Fire Next Time*.

Coming home by BART from a reading in Oakland, I tell Yedda and Jocelyn that I've been struggling with my writing, which had then just begun to emerge from my early engagement with the reports. I confess a fear of my poems' indecency *wrong object choice* but the truth is that I'm more suspicious of my own haunting feeling of wrongness, as if there were an ethical imperative to preserve a radical difference *between soldier and detainee* to respect a mystified distinction whose breach would open my writing to violence and shame. To eroticize the wounds of a soldier is one thing, I say, voicing some imagined admonition, but to sexualize *exploit* the body of a hunger-striking detainee crosses a line. To critique extrajudicial detention *or any form of incarceration* is one thing, I say, but to make the detainee's body the common place of my devotional kink is like ripping a hole in his corpse in order to go on fucking it.

Later that month, after publicly broaching some of these anxieties for the first time at Sophie's series of Poem Talks at the n/a gallery, Lara asks me how I'm able to sexualize the already violated body in my poems, a question I can't stop asking myself, and I wonder with her whether there's another way to feel my relation to his body except by way of sensory mediation and subjective arousal. If his body has already been repressively sexualized in our militarized unconscious, is there any way to make that operation perceptible *if only to myself* except thru the sensual participation of *my* body? I don't know and I can't adequately answer these questions. I only want to wrest his body away from the use to which it's been assigned, to turn the uselessness of waste into the uselessness of pleasure, to feel his visceral opacity in such a way that abolishes a mystified relation without idealizing it. Maybe I need to feel these contradictions as they pierce my skin.

But the desire is not for sex. It is rather to feel any relation whatever. As I struggle to overcompensate for a negated intimacy, my default to the sexual *reflex, tic* allows me to perceive the enclosed horizon that impedes any other economy of bodies and pleasures. Even as it explodes its usefulness *hygienic reproduction and domestic security* sex fails to transgress its containment.

Jill's question a year later feels equally consequential. Doesn't my insistence on the homoerotic amplify masculinist prerogatives at the expense of so many gendered relations around extraordinary rendition, relations totally eclipsed here? Women left behind in villages, women involved in detention, interrogation, treatment, feeding, and care. The question is a source of some embarrassment as I have no satisfying answer. The best I can do is to say that I want my poems to be like sensory organs becoming "theoreticians immediately in their praxis" (Marx) making seemingly abstract relations perceptible thru concrete sensation and if these new organs can only be extensions of my particular body then I can only respond to whatever eros arouses my senses. And while this eros is inseparable from my personal history, it also has a gendered history to which I am subject.

When I share my anxieties about these autopsy poems with Bruce, he allays my worries by emphasizing how the erotic always shares kinship with compassion, a way of thinking informed by his Buddhist practice. It's just a matter of scale, or corporeal proximity, he says, like the coming together of discrete beings in the recognition of suffering *separation*. But I'm afraid I can't claim for my eroticization of the detainee's body the compassion that Bruce wants to inspire. Can I even presume to recognize his suffering? Or would such a presumption *bad faith of good conscience* be as repellant as the detention that conditions it?

Striking a similar note on our drive home from the gallery talk, Camille continues the conversation, suggesting that the autopsy report materializes a kind of negative space. Compassion is born in just such a space, she says, and I'm struck by how much sense this makes insofar as the report is where the body is shorn *equalized & substitutable* relieved of its social artifice. This is the space wherein to feel his body is to feel *any* body, its specificity universalized at the same time as it's negated. Not being a thing seen, his body is the invisible light by which things become visible. It points the way *a hole in the weave of perception* where I become his shadow as he slumbers in our speech and dreams me here.

But compassion is not so easily won, Emily reminds me, because compassion's condition of possibility is the other's singularity with which one can neither identify nor relate and whose marks on the body *effects of social force* are liquidated in the space of the report.

And so I can only long for the inconceivable, to lift his unremarkable genitalia away from the exceptional death to which they've been consigned and to turn the common place toward its negated material, a hole in the public sphere *black site of suffering* where everything social flickers before vanishing.

Maybe this is what I mean by love, the failure of my name for you. And if this tenderness is true it will shatter the truth that excludes it, realizing my heresy by exhausting every identity in glamour and void.

March 2013 – December 2014
San Francisco and Ypsilanti

ACKNOWLEDGMENTS

Some of these poems, or versions thereof, appeared in the following publications: *Dreamboat, Materials, Boston Review, The Claudius App, Tripwire, Number Two, The Volta, Fourteen Hills, Sundial, Elderly, Loose Change,* and *The White Review*. "To Burn With Love (A Suite)" first appeared in *Chicago Review*. "Late Nite Emissions" appears in its entirety in *Animal Shelter* (Semiotext(e)), with the editorial guidance of Robert Dewhurst. "Hocus-Pocus (I)" appears online at *Public Access*, designed by Nicholas Grider. "House-Scrub, or After Porn" appears as a limited edition chapbook designed and published by Margaret Tedesco and 2nd Floor Projects. Deepest thanks to all the editors and publishers for their support.

Common Place finds its point of departure in a 2009 U.S. Armed Forces autopsy report of a Yemeni man detained at Guantanamo. Many of the pieces metabolize that document, while drawing on other texts: "Evidence of Injury" rewrites Walt Whitman's, "I Sing the Body Electric." "Funeral Rites" moves through several passages of Jean Genet's novel of the same title. "Open Up a Few Corpses" periodically scores language from the chapter of the same title in Michel Foucault's *Birth of the Clinic* as well as A.R. Thomas's *The Practical Guide for Making Post-Mortem Examinations and for the*

Study of Morbid Anatomy (1873). "Flashback" adapts a document marked, "SECRET || NOFORN || 20330610 Department of Defense Headquarters, Joint Task Force, Guantanamo U.S. Naval Station, Guantanamo Bay, Cuba 10 June 2008," accessed through WikiLeaks. "Abundance Washed" builds on several sentences adapted from the Marquis de Sade's *120 Days of Sodom* and Simone de Beauvoir's "Must We Burn Sade?," while also quoting Alice Notley's "Self '78 Speak." "Contribution to a Critique of My Philosophy of Ardor" rewrites the final paragraphs of Karl Marx's "Contribution to the Critique of Hegel's *Philosophy of Right*: Introduction." The title of "As For Myself In the Present" is lifted from the final page of Bruce Boone's *Century of Clouds*; and "un tombeau vide en extase courbeé," which concludes that piece, quotes Baudelaire's poem "Le Cygne." Christian Hawkey's kind engagement with "Nocturnal Residua" enabled the completion of that poem-essay. The phrase "noiseless white void" appearing in the same piece is borrowed from an imprisoned poet with whom I work at Women's Huron Valley Correctional Facility in Ypsilanti, Michigan. "Devotional Kink" was motivated by an invitation from curator Sophie Dahlin to give a "Poem Talk" at the n/a Gallery in Oakland (June 2013). Gratitude to my many interlocutors who appear here by name—Caleb Smith, Lara Durback, Camille Roy, Bruce Boone, Bob Glück, Robbie Dewhurst, Jill Richards, Emily Abendroth, Brian Whitener, Lewis

Freedman, Anna Vitale, Dana Ward, Joseph Bradshaw, Ted Rees, Yedda Morrison, Jocelyn Saidenberg, Melissa Jones, Matvei Yankelevich, Mary Poole and David Chapman—as well as the many friends whose engagement with the work impacted its core.

Anna Moschovakis believed in *Common Place* long before it had arrived, and without whose care, together with that of Michael Newton at UDP, this book would not be what it is.

Infinite appreciation to those who patiently listened to this writing while it was still in progress and whose questions and comments nourished and pushed the work in ways I never could have done by myself—especially Lee, who has heard it all so many times and never ceased to respond. Special thanks to Michael Cross for guidance as sure as the North Star.

Rob Halpern lives between San Francisco and Ypsilanti, Michigan, where he teaches at Eastern Michigan University and Huron Valley Women's Correctional Facility. *Common Place* is his fourth volume of poetry after *Music for Porn*, *Disaster Suites*, and *Rumored Place*, all of which, together, comprise an ongoing work. Together with Taylor Brady, Halpern also co-authored *Snow Sensitive Skin*. *[——] Placeholder*, a book-length selection of his poetry and prose drawn from across all of these books, was published in the UK in 2015.